LECTIO MATTERS

Matters Series

Lectio Matters

Before the Burning Bush

Mary Margaret Funk, OSB

LITURGICAL PRESS
Collegeville, Minnesota

www.litpress.org

Deep gratitude to our prioress, Sister Juliann Babcock, OSB; my Benedictine community of Our Lady of Grace Monastery in Beech Grove, Indiana; and my Irish Cistercian sisters, Abbess Marie Fahy, OCSO, and nuns of St. Mary's Abbey in Glencairn, County Waterford. This set revision of the Matters Series is because of the vision and competence of Hans Christoffersen and staff at Liturgical Press, Collegeville, Minnesota.

Cover design by Jodi Hendrickson. Cover image: "Moses at the Burning Bush," by Eastern Orthodox Nun Rebecca Cown of New Skete, Cambridge, New York. Commissioned by Pamela Farris. Based on an original at the Monastery of St. Catherine, Mount Sinai, Egypt. Used by permission.

Excerpts from the English translation of *Rite of Penance* © 1974, International Commission on English in the Liturgy Corporation (ICEL); excerpts from the English translation of *The Roman Missal* © 2010, ICEL. All rights reserved.

From *A Better Wine*, edited by Kevin Culligan, OCD, copyright © Washington Province of Discalced Carmelites, Inc., ICS Publications, 2131 Lincoln Road, NE, Washington, DC, 20002-1199; www.icspublications.org.

Book of Jonah, trans. Abbot Laurence O'Keefe, OSB, St Augustine's Abbey, Ramsgate, Kent, CT11 9PA, England, 2009.

Story of Lectio of Experience by Kathleen Cahalan, PhD.

Scripture texts in this work are taken from the *New Revised Standard Version Bible* © 1989, Division of Christian Education of the National Council of the Churches of Christ in the United States of America. Used by permission. All rights reserved.

2	3	4	5	6	7	8

Library of Congress Cataloging-in-Publication Data

Funk, Mary Margaret.
    Lectio matters : before the burning bush / Mary Margaret Funk, OSB.—Revised edition
        p.   cm.
    Includes bibliographical references (pages   ).
    ISBN 978-0-8146-3505-6 — ISBN 978-0-8146-3491-2 (e-book)
    1. Bible—Reading.   2. Bible—Devotional use.   3. Bible OT—Devotional use.   I. Title.

BS617.F86   2012
224'.9206—dc23   2012039187

To my guardian angel,
Brigid Funk,
who shows up from time to time
when lectio *matters!*

Contents

"Moses at the Burning Bush," by Eastern Orthodox Nun
Rebecca Cown of New Skete, Cambridge, NY,
commissioned by Pamela Farris, based on an original at
the Monastery of St. Catherine, Mount Sinai, Egypt

Iconographer's Preface

Rebecca Cown

By means of all created things, without exception,
The Divine assails us, penetrates us, and molds us.
We imagine it as distant and inaccessible.
In fact, we live steeped in its burning layers.
—Teilhard de Chardin

One of the pillars of spiritual teaching in Eastern Christianity is deification (Greek: *theosis*),[1] which means participating or sharing in the divine nature. This is our inheritance, according to St. Dorotheus of Gaza; it is an inborn spark of divinity like a light burning deep within our hearts, within the core of our being, guiding us as we discern what pleases God, and illuminating our journey upon this earth. Christ speaks about this same light when he says we are not to hide our light under a bushel but bring it into the light of day. In this broken world, however, this inner light, this divine sensation, is often covered up by the cares and concerns of our daily lives and by our conditioning from early childhood. St. Paul also speaks about this enlightenment and the need to stay awake, to become conscious and aware—not simply about the life of our outer senses, but especially about our interior senses.[2] We call this the light of discernment. Another term is *aesthesis*, a Greek word difficult to translate into English, which we may understand as inner perception or divine sensation: a spiritual sense. Our innermost spiritual senses need to be made conscious and honed and practiced in our daily lives.

Our earliest Christian teachers reiterated that "God became human in order that the human person may become God." This divine gift presupposes our personal and collective inner work, our synergy with God. This potential has been present from the very beginning, according to the account in Genesis, since we are created in the image and likeness of God. The "image" is the reflection of God. One commentary on this Genesis passage says that "likeness" refers to being endowed with discernment and understanding. So, by inference, we might say that the "likeness" is what we are called to bring into reality by inner discernment.

St. Gregory of Nazianzus says, "Whatever is not consciously embraced cannot be transformed." That is, unless we awaken to this divine reality in our hearts, to who we really are and to what we are called, we cannot engage with this Divine Spirit within, and it will remain dormant. We are personally called to be transformed and transfigured into our God-likeness, but not just for our-selves; we are called personally to become God's agents and to enable God's ongoing creation of this world of ours.[3]

God has no other hands, feet, eyes, mind, or heart than ours to continue God's creating. The Spirit of God is everywhere present and filling all things, and human beings have been called to cocreate with God. The raw materials, so to speak, need our working with God to bring about life, harmony, peace, justice, and beauty out of chaos and disorder. God has given us the mission and purpose of incarnating God's very first words—"Let there be Light"—and to make it a living reality in our lives.

The story of Moses before the burning bush may well be a paradigm of every person's divine visitation or awak-ening to the divine presence. If heeded, this encoun-ter will change a person's life. This change, or *metanoia* (Greek for "change of heart," "change of purpose, direc-tion"), moves us away from our former identity, where the ego is in control, to become an instrument in God's hand. This is what happened to Moses, who once was a Hebrew slave, saved by an Egyptian princess. He was raised and educated as an adopted prince but later, hav-ing slain an Egyptian overseer, fled for his life into a foreign land and then became a shepherd. After many years in this lonely desert, God revealed to Moses his true identity and purpose in life.

The story tells us that Moses was tending the flock of Jethro, his father-in-law, and led the flock to the far side of the desert. He came to Horeb, the mountain of God. There, the angel of the Lord appeared to him in flames of fire from within a thorn bush. Moses saw that, although the bush was on fire, it was not consumed. So Moses thought, "I will go over and see this strange sight—why the bush is not burnt." When the Lord saw that Moses had gone over to look, God called to him from within the bush: "Moses! Moses!"

And Moses said, "Here I am."

"Do not come any closer," God said. "Take off your sandals, for the place where you are standing is holy ground." Then he said, "I am the God of your father, the God of Abraham, the God of Isaac, and the God of Jacob." At this, Moses hid his face because he was afraid to look at God.

The icon on the cover of this book depicts this encounter. Several aspects of the icon highlight our journey toward discernment. First, the bush is actually a thorn bush, typical of the desert, indicating that there isn't any place where God cannot be encountered! Next, we see the blackened sandals behind Moses. Sandals are made of the skin of animals; they are dead skins, indicating the passing nature of our persona, our identity in this world. Moses puts behind him his sense of who he has been; without it, he is vulnerable and full of fear. Yet, the icon manifests his readiness to follow the call into an unknown, to a mysterious and awesome divine encounter. His ego identity is not in control. The icon also indicates a change in his consciousness of who he really is. His clothing is radiant with divine light. His ego is not obliterated but participates in the Light of God. He has awakened to the divine spark within, to his true identity in God. His inner senses are illumined, awakened, and he hears the voice of God telling him to lead his people out of Egypt.[4]

What ensues is a dialogue with God. Moses' first reaction is "Who am I?" Stripped of his former security in who he thought he was, he now is aware of his limitations, his sense of inadequacy. But his former identity doesn't just totally disappear; for now it will become God's agent in responding to the plight of his people. God assures him, "I will be with you." To us as to Moses, this is the invitation to center our attention on a new identity—on God consciousness, on a God who is full of compassion.

After the divine awakening comes the descent into the daily: the call for us to incarnate ("en-flesh") God's presence in this broken world. We perceive Moses' resistance, his difficulty in accepting the challenge of being God's instrument in the liberation of his people. He is *invited* by God; this mission is not forced upon him! The experience gives him the light, the strength, the discernment to face the challenges, to face his own fears, his resistances, and his limitations in fulfilling the divine mission—which is also his own purpose.

We see Moses at the foot of the holy mountain. Mount Horeb is at the bottom; the summit is Sinai, which Moses will later ascend and where he will commune with God in the deepest recesses of his being. This present encounter is his new beginning. Enlightenment is not a place where we build a tent and savor God's presence in bliss for the rest of our lives. Nevertheless, it is a divine light.

When Meg asked me to write this preface, my very first thought was a certain sense that whoever is drawn to this book has most certainly already experienced something akin to Moses' visitation (or theophany, as Eastern Christians may say). In other words, one who is drawn or deeply attracted to God must surely be responding from a God-given divine sensation, the inner light I mentioned at the beginning of this essay. Our experience may not be as dramatic as Moses' or St. Paul's experience, but even if it is more subtle, it is nonetheless real. It is one thing, however, to experience this divine presence and another to flesh it out in our lives. This process requires serious reflection on the tools for the spiritual journey. Who am I? What am I called to by God? How do I discern the path ahead? Discernment grows as we are purified in all the areas of our being.

In these times, when spiritual guides and teachers are often inaccessible, this book may well be a companion on the journey, one that will support us through what may feel like a labyrinth or a maze as we make our way through the complexities of everyday life and the seasons of more profound changes. Just as Moses in the desert received what he needed to discern his new life, these writings by Meg Funk offer tools for growth in self-knowledge, for deepening our relationship to God, and for growing in discernment with God consciousness in our own life and purpose.

Rebecca Cown
New Skete
Cambridge, New York

Foreword

Who is the hero of the book of Jonah? Not Jonah himself, for he is, at best, an awkward instrument in the hands of God when given his commission to preach conversion to the people of Nineveh. Could it be the great fish which swallows the prophet, thus giving him a second chance to carry out the call of God? We all need second chances, and sometimes such a means is provided to take us back to where we were before.

Or could it even be the people of Nineveh who, unlike Jonah, respond to God's word immediately and so undergo a complete conversion? In fact, the real hero is God himself. He it is who initiates every action: the Hebrew word *manah* ("appoint") is used of God four times in the book, moving the story forward, as well as calling Jonah to go to Nineveh, which he does twice.

But one can also think of the hero of the book as oneself. In *lectio divina*, you open yourself to the working of God, almost becoming part of the sacred text for God to speak in the deepest part of your being, what Scripture calls the heart. In this book you will accompany the author, Sister Mary Margaret, who will unfold to you the various levels of *lectio divina*. She uses the book of Jonah as an illustration of how to approach Scripture, so that it becomes a real encounter with the living God. She gives you not only an in-depth study of *lectio* but, more important, some guidance on how to go about it.

The cover of the book has a striking image—an icon of Moses before the burning bush. This is instructive, for that phenomenon which attracted Moses on Mount Sinai turned an ordinary day into an extraordinary one, and Moses from being a murderer and a fugitive into the deliverer and lawgiver of the people of Israel. It is the same God whom we encounter in our *lectio*, revealing to us who we are, and what it is that God wants of us.

With great skill, Sister Meg shows how *lectio* is related to the spiritual life, as taught by the ancient church writers, especially Cassian. Much of this teaching she has already given us in her previous books, especially *Thoughts Matter*, which, she tells us, took her ten years to write, so distilling her wisdom and experience for us.

More recent writers are not overlooked. In her book *Humility Matters* she gives us the teaching of both St. Teresa of Jesus and St. Thérèse of Lisieux, both of whom have that honorable title of Doctor of the Church. Sister Meg has given us the benefit of her own experience of growth through *lectio*, making this book a very personal one, to which the reader can so easily relate. She shows how life's experiences are a form of *lectio*, to find sermons in stones, as Shakespeare puts it—a sentiment also found four centuries before him in St. Bernard.

"Did not our hearts burn within us, as he spoke to us on the way?" said the two disciples at Emmaus.

On your life's journey may this book make such a fire burn within you until you, like them, recognize the presence of the Lord in the reading of the Scriptures and the breaking of the bread.

Abbot Laurence O'Keefe, OSB

Introduction

Lectio **Matters:**
Before the Burning Bush

As a child I knew how to pray. It seems like as an adult I lost that natural, soft, abiding awareness both of myself and of God. I don't remember when this habitual consciousness thinned out, but I knew God was missing in my life and I needed to return to this home base as my number one priority. In 1961, at the age of eighteen, I entered the monastery. It took many years but I found again that childlike personal way of praying to God through *lectio divina*.

Recently, Pope Benedict XVI recommended this for all the faithful:

> I would like in particular to recall and recommend the ancient tradition of *lectio divina*: the diligent reading of Sacred Scripture accompanied by prayer brings about that intimate dialogue in which the person reading

hears God who is speaking, and in praying, responds to him with trusting openness of heart. If the practice of *lectio divina* is effectively promoted, I am convinced that it will bring to the church a new spiritual springtime.[1]

This book is my experience of seeking God through the ancient tradition recommended by St. Benedict. His directive in the Rule is to do *lectio divina* several hours each day.[2] When his directives are carried out, it seems to me that we are asked to do *lectio* whenever we are not doing something else. Though I love the choir and the common life in the monastery with the other sisters, I feel that this personal time for prayer and silence is necessary for me to live the monastic way of life. Through regular, long hours of silence, my habit of remembering God is restored time after time to the way it was when I was a child on that Benton County farm in Northern Indiana.

Now, after fifty years of being a nun, I would like to share with others who are also inclined toward this way of praying through *lectio*. The pages that follow present how I have learned to do *lectio* and how I teach others to do this kind of prayer through a sustained practice of *lectio divina*. First, I begin with a description of the method; then I provide a practical example from Scripture. I will share my recent experience of doing *lectio* using the book of Jonah. Scripture has the most theory about what *lectio* is and how to do it, but many may be called to listen to other revelatory texts, not from Scripture, but from experience or nature. I have included another example from the book of life that weaves through the revelatory text of Scripture: *lectio* on experience is probably the way most people find God. Kathleen Cahalan, PhD, shares her sustained *lectio* in this book. Life experience is her first teacher and Scripture is a witness to what has already happened in her life. She's an example to me that many Christians are already doing *lectio divina* but discover the language in the tradition after having already lived it in their ordinary lives. In this sense, we don't need to learn how to do *lectio*, we only need this language to know what it is we are doing when we do it. We need each other to encourage us to sustain this inner work, not from time to time, but as a way of life.

Again, we know that sustained *lectio* can be sourced from one of three texts: the book of Holy Scripture, the book of experience, or the book of nature. For this book, *Lectio Matters*, I will teach the method of *lectio divina* through the book of Scripture, using the book of Jonah. All these revelatory texts bring us to our knees. We take our shoes off. We are each like Moses before the burning bush.

The Method of Sustained *Lectio Divina*

Lectio divina is a sustained immersion into a revelatory text. While Scripture is the classic revelation of encounter with God, the text could be from other sources like a personal event from the book of life or an experience from the book of nature.

Lectio divina is an encounter with God:

1. through the revelatory text of nature, experience, or Scripture
2. mediated by the voices of the text: literal, symbolic, moral, mystical[3]
3. we receive through the senses of the reader: logical, intuitive, ascetical (personal), spiritual[4]

Lectio divina is a way of praying using the revelatory texts of Scripture, nature, or experience.

This encounter with God is to listen with the ear of our heart. *Lectio divina* is our burning bush. We take off our sandals and bow our brow to the ground: our being bends low before the living God.

We invoke the Holy Spirit to bring to mind our particular text to use for *lectio divina* in the coming months. We linger with this text for months, or until another text rises from underneath our conscious awareness.

- We listen to the literal voice of the text and study with our logical mind.
- We meditate on the symbolic voice of the text with our intuitive mind (aesthetical).
- We heed the moral voice of God with our personal senses of prayer and ascetical practices. We comply with this inner voice through our daily decisions and through the discipline of discernment.
- We receive the mystical voice with our spiritual senses.

Each of these voices is distinct and is mediated through the revelatory text. Our part in this encounter is to listen, meditate, heed with discrimination, and receive the impulse of the Holy Spirit.

This way of personal prayer becomes our way of life, a culture of God consciousness.

This method depends on the Holy Spirit enlightening our mind and filling our heart with desire. The text is given to us as an individual and each of us takes the necessary days, weeks, and months to live into the revelation. This is sustained *lectio*.

Skills of study, artistic appreciation, training of the mind for discipline, and the disposition of repentance prepare us for the deepest experience of the encounter with God before the burning bush.

Discernment becomes a way of life. We do this *lectio* as our default way of living in the world. We do this practice when we are not doing anything else. This *lectio* is the culture under the river of our interior life that provides us with directives of how to be loving above the river to all, especially the least among us.[5]

Lectio divina is an encounter with the living God within our loving heart. This is our individual practice that prepares us for liturgy, selfless service, community life, friendships, and an ecclesial way of being in the world. Sustained *lectio divina* is a way of life. Rather than a formal exercise of an hour a day, *lectio* is what we do all day long.[6]

The Alexandrian Catechetical School promoted study of the literal sense because, unlike the Greek myth system, the Christian story had a human Jesus who was also God. He was the Christ who fulfilled the Hebrew Scriptures. The teachers from Alexandria did exegesis on the literal level of the text but went on to specialize in teaching the spiritual senses of Scripture. They not only communicated information about this event but also transmitted the Good News as a revelation. Scripture had not only a literal sense (which could also be historical) but also an allegorical sense, a moral sense, and an anagogical sense (movement toward contemplation).[7]

Later this richness of allegory and mystical interpretations comes to us through St. Benedict. His rule, possibly written about 520 CE, is a masterful anthology of the scholars and saints who taught during those first four hundred years of Christianity after the death of the apostles. The influence of the Alexandrian Catechetical School is embedded in the Rule of Benedict. Monks were taught a mystical way of interpretation as well as a diligent scientific exegesis of Scripture.[8] Benedict wanted his monks to be immersed in the Bible and provided hours every day for this work.

When we started the Beech Grove School of *Lectio Divina* in 2000, we found it helpful as a teaching method to separate the voice of the text from the reader's senses. This innovation is compatible with tradition.[9] In English, the word "senses" is used both for the text and for the reader and therefore causes confusion. So instead of using the word "senses" for the text, we use the word "voice." For the reader, we use the word "senses" as receptors of the words of the text. There are more voices and more senses in inspired literature, but these four voices (literal, symbolic, moral, mystical) received by four senses (literal, allegorical, moral, anagogical) will provide a little method to go deeply and devoutly into contemplative prayer.

We begin our sustained *lectio divina* with earnest prayer: *epiclesis.* Come, Holy Spirit, come. We know not how to pray as we ought but groan in eager expectation. First, we devote ourselves to prayer so that (a) the text is revealed to us and (b) we are open to receive.

There are three revelatory texts: nature, experience, and Scripture. We wait upon the Lord to reveal to us the text that is our invitation and what is on the other side of the door that invites us to this sustained *lectio*. The universal prayer form is the Liturgy of the Eucharist, or Mass. The common prayer form is the Divine Office. *Lectio divina* is the traditional individual prayer form.[10] No one can do this for us. If we are not doing it, we, as monastics, do not fulfill the directive of St. Benedict to do *lectio divina*.

Notice this is not a group activity but our individual supplication: I pray. I discern which door of the revelatory text is being revealed to me and what will be my *lectio divina* for the next several months of practice. "O God, come to my assistance; O Lord, make haste to help me" (Ps 70:1).

Each of us will have a unique theme, but we share the same journey as we go deeper and deeper into the revelation of mystery. The element of surprise and delight is a sign that the Holy Spirit is "at work" within and among us as a community.

Epiclesis: *Prayer of Invocation to the Holy Spirit*

First, I call the Holy Spirit to come down, overshadow me, quicken my mind, and warm my heart. I ask for guidance about where to start and what text to use; finally, I ask the Spirit to provide the grace to remove obstacles that hinder me in my resolve.

My entry-level initiative is to pray to the Holy Spirit.

Epiclesis is a Greek word meaning "to call down." The *epiclesis* is to ask, like the priest does at eucharistic liturgy, the Holy Spirit to "Make holy, therefore, these gifts, we pray, by sending down your Spirit upon them like the dewfall, so that they may become for us the Body and Blood of our Lord Jesus Christ."[11] According to the pre–Vatican II rubrics, at this point of the liturgy, a bell was to be rung and the priest was to place his hands over the bread and the wine. This signaled the faithful to kneel down before the mystery. This is the preparation before the priest pronounces the words of consecration.

We do the same in our individual prayer as at eucharistic liturgy. We invoke the Holy Spirit to come down and be with us as we start our *lectio divina* prayer. This is continuing the prayers at our eucharistic liturgy where there is a second *epiclesis* ("invocation upon") when the priest begs the Father to send the Holy Spirit, the Sanctifier, so that the offerings may become the Body and Blood of Christ and that the faithful, by receiving them, may become a living offering to God.[12] The goal of *lectio divina* is to indeed become that living offering to God through Christ as we pray every day at Mass.

St. Benedict says that whenever we begin anything we begin with earnest prayer.[13] As you see, *lectio divina* is a prayer, and we place ourselves under this dove that is hovering. As we know from Scripture, the Spirit hovered over the waters in the Genesis creation account and in the overshadowing events in the New Testament: Jesus' baptism, the transfiguration, Mary's annunciation, and Pentecost. As we want to be quickened in our *lectio*, we linger here and invoke the Holy Spirit to come, inspire, dwell, abide, and let not the word return void.

You might ask, "How do we do this prayer? Is it a single prayer of supplication?" We do not know how to pray. That is why we need the Spirit to come and teach us.

So, as I gather my *lectio* revelatory text, I stand humble and ready. I watch and pray. Usually the text is right before my eyes. I had been into it for days, weeks, even years, this desire for God and a willingness to do whatever it took to find the Presence that I remember having as a child. I lift up this prayer like a dove soars to the heavens. I then dive deeply into the mystical stream of my Catholic tradition.

The text came: be simple. Take this little book seriously. Engage in the book of Jonah. I was trained to be a perpetual student. I doubted that such a little book would teach me much about Scripture or be deep and wide enough for a long, lingering *lectio*, but I also felt a growing fatigue with reading. In my era of religious life, we were saturated with spiritual reading. I simply consumed book after book, and books, and then I read books about the books I read. The more I read, the less satisfied I became. Was I swimming in the direction of God, toward a contemplative life in prayer?

I asked for a confirming sign to trust my invitation to be content with a long, lingering look at the book of Jonah. I felt called to do an ascetical practice before I could hear God's directive about my invitation to *lectio*: I put boundaries on my reading of magazines, newspapers, newsletters, advertisements, the glut of paper that comes to me from all sides. I glanced but refrained from reading. I took care that watching television and listening to podcasts on my iPhone were in service of my *lectio* and not temptations away from it. In short, I emptied my mind of the flood of media.[14]

I opened my Bible to the book of Jonah.[15]

I felt that God is merciful; if I took up the wrong text or event, our Lord would guide my heart to find the right place. I felt I didn't want a mind full of current events; I wanted to seek God and put on the mind of Christ. After this *epiclesis* moment of asking and receiving in faith my revelatory text, I got started. *Lectio divina* is reading God.

You might wonder what was my confirming sign both to do *lectio* with the book of Jonah and also to report about my practice of *lectio* in this book. The book of Jonah first came to me from a practical point of view, as a good teaching tool. It was short, dramatic, and densely instructive. Then I realized that Jonah had been an abiding metaphor for me. I saw the text no longer as a teaching tool for others but as a necessary transmission for my spiritual journey. My confirming sign was a realization of a pattern of my own recurring experience of setting out in one direction, getting washed out, then spending deep down time, like Jonah in the whale.

It seems to me that often I would embark on a mission of this or that and get turned back rather dramatically. Three times I felt called to do something. Went. And three times I was washed overboard and returned to my Indiana monastery (Catholic University, Bolivia, Ireland). I never considered myself to be a prophet, but certainly I felt that I was called to do the will of God. Over and over again, though, I found life's events shifted me back from this or that false start. Also, I found the audiences to which I was sent to be far more in touch with God than I was. Nineveh converted me over and over again.

Another confirming sign was to have an eye condition that lasted about eighteen months. For one year, I could neither read nor drive a car. I could, however, see in my mind's eye the whole book of Jonah. I actually felt swallowed and parked in the belly of a great fish with impending darkness for the rest of my life, but, thanks to Dr. Tom Funk, I had a surgery that returned almost my full sight. But this gets ahead of my story here about teaching this sustained method of *lectio divina*. I consider writing this book to be a great privilege. This book, *Lectio Matters:*

Before the Burning Bush, refrains from talking about *lectio*; instead, I hope to encourage doing the practice of *lectio*.

Voices and Senses

There are many ways of doing *lectio divina*.[16] The method I use is a contemporary version of what I would have learned if I were a student in the Alexandrian Catechetical School that goes back to the fourth century. This early theological school taught the voices of the text. Living in the twenty-first century, I realize that different parts of my mind receive a voice specifically designed to fit certain parts of my brain. I consider how a reader, such as myself, receives the different voices. I use a different part of my brain to figure out the plain voice. I use other parts of my brain that decodes the symbolic voice. The text may have as many as four voices or may use one of the distinct voices that requires the reader's specific senses designed to receive that particular voice:

1) The literal voice is studied by the logical senses of the mind (left brain).
2) The symbolic (allegorical) voice is received by the intuitive senses of the mind (right brain).
3) The moral voice is heard by the personal senses that heed the directives of the voice (I come to my personal senses and take action because the directive comes from God and is intended for me). The moral voice comes through my own voice, but as I get more attuned to hearing this moral voice, I

can distinguish the promptings from the voice of the Holy Spirit.

4) The mystical voice is the experience of God that simply rises from within when purity of heart reigns. This voice is received by the spiritual senses. Just like our physical senses, we have eyes, ears, touch receptors that get the message with wonderful proportion, delight, and surprise.

This method of *lectio divina* is an encounter with the living God.

If this seems daunting, be at peace. *Lectio divina* is simply a way we humans have of knowing and loving. Prayer is natural and has its own inherent symmetry. After all, prayer is our personal relationship with God who made us—and made us with a huge desire for the deepest life lived in our Creator.

Chapter 1

The Text of the Book of Jonah: The Actual Reading of the Text

First, let's read the entire text as a whole.[1]

The Book of Jonah

Chapter 1

The Word of the Lord came to Jonah the Son of Amittai.
"Get up: go to Nineveh the great city,
preach against it, for the evil it has done has come up
   before me."
Jonah rose to run away to Tarshish, from the Lord.
He went down to Joppa and found a ship bound for
   Tarshish.
He paid his fare and went aboard to go with them to
   Tarshish far away from the Lord.
Then the Lord hurled a great wind upon the sea,
and such a fierce storm that they thought that the ship
   would break up.

The sailors were afraid, and each one prayed aloud to
   his god.
They threw the ship's cargo into the sea, to lighten it,
but Jonah went below deck, lay down, and fell asleep.
The ship's captain came to him and said:
"Get up: why are you still sleeping? Pray to your God.
Perhaps he will take notice of us so that we do not die."
They said to one another:
"Come, let us cast lots to know whose fault it is that
   this disaster has come upon us."
They cast lots, and Jonah was singled out.
They said: "Tell us why this disaster has overtaken us.
What is your occupation? Where do you come from?
From which country? From which people?"
He answered: "I am a Hebrew. I worship the Lord of
   heaven,
who created the sea and the dry land."
The men were greatly afraid,
for he told them that he was running away from the
   presence of the Lord.
They asked him, "What ought we to do to you
to make the sea calm again?"
For the sea was growing more and more stormy.
He said: "Take me and throw me into the sea
and it will become calm.
For I know that it is because of me that this storm has
   come upon you."
The men rowed to get back to dry land, but they could
   not

for the sea grew more and more stormy against them.
Then they prayed to the Lord:
"Let us not perish because of this man's life
nor regard us as guilty for shedding his blood.
For you have done as it pleased you."
Then they took Jonah and threw him into the sea.
And the sea ceased to rage.
The men revered the Lord greatly.
They offered sacrifice and made vows.

Chapter 2

The Lord prepared a great fish to swallow Jonah.
He was inside the fish for three days and three nights.
Jonah prayed to the Lord his God from inside the fish.
He said:
"In my suffering I cried to the Lord, and he answered me.
From the depths of the grave I cried for help
and you heard my voice.
You threw me into the deep, into the heart of the seas.
The flood surrounded me,
all your breakers and waves passed over me."
He said: "I am rejected from your presence,
I will never again look on your holy temple.
The waters surrounded me up to my throat,
The deep surrounded me, weeds twisted round my head.
I went down to the very bases of the mountains,
the gates of the Underworld closed upon me,
yet you raised me up from the pit, O Lord my God.
My life was fainting away, then I remembered the Lord.

My prayer came before you into your holy temple.
Those who revere empty idols forsake the mercy shown
    them.
As for me, I will sacrifice to you with loud thanksgiving,
and repay you what I have vowed."
The Lord spoke to the fish, and it vomited up Jonah
    onto the dry land.

Chapter 3

Then the word of the Lord came to Jonah a second time.
"Get up: go to that great city Nineveh
and proclaim to it the message I am telling you."
Jonah arose and went to Nineveh according to the
    word of the Lord.
Now Nineveh was a great city—it would take three
    days to walk through it.
Jonah began to go through the city; it took him one day.
He proclaimed: "In forty days' time Nineveh will be
    overthrown."
The men of Nineveh believed God and proclaimed a fast.
Both small and great put on sackcloth.
Word came to the King of Nineveh;
he rose from his throne, took off his robe of state,
and sat in ashes.
A proclamation was made throughout Nineveh.
"By the decree of the King and his court
no one is to taste anything: not even the animals,
oxen or sheep, shall taste anything.
They shall not be pastured, or drink any water.

Everybody—men and animals—must put on sackcloth
and make fervent prayers to God.
Everyone should turn from his evil way of life
and from the violence which he does.
Who knows—perhaps God will change his mind and
feel sorry for us,
turn from his wrath, so that we do not perish."
God saw what they did,
how they turned from their evil way of life.
He changed his mind about what he would do to
them, and did not do it.

Chapter 4

Jonah took this very badly and became angry.
He prayed to the Lord and said,
"O Lord, isn't this what I said when I was in my own
land?
That is why I ran away to Tarshish that first time.
I know that you are a merciful and compassionate God,
patient, and full of kindness, ever changing your mind
about doing harm.
Now, Lord, I might as well die, for to me death is better
than life."
The Lord said, "Is it a good thing for you to be angry?"
Jonah went out of the city, and sat down at the east of it.
He made for himself a shelter, and sat in its shade
to see what would become of the city.
The Lord made a little plant and made it grow up over
Jonah

so as to shade his head, to keep him from any discomfort.
Jonah was very glad about the little plant.
The Lord made a maggot at dawn the next day
which attacked the plant so it withered away.
When the sun rose, the Lord made a scorching east wind.
The sun beat down upon Jonah's head, and he grew
   faint.
He wanted to die, and said, "Death is better than life."
The Lord said, "Is it a good thing for you to be angry
   about the little plant?"
Jonah answered, "Yes, angry enough to die!"
The Lord said "You feel sorry for the little plant,
yet you did not do any work for it or make it grow.
It existed for a day then came to an end in a night.
Should I not feel sorry for Nineveh, that great city,
in which there are more than twenty thousand people
   who do not know right from wrong,
as well as many animals?"

Chapter 2

The Literal Voice Studied by the Logical Senses of the Mind

Meg's Study of the Literal Voice

I study the literal voice of the text using my logical mind. With my Bible open, I read the introduction, some study helps, the text. I check the footnotes and the annotation references; I do the cross-referencing leisurely. Maybe I read the whole of the book that was suggested in the reference. For example, I read another prophet, like Jeremiah, to see how Jonah is different or the same. I have marked my Bible for further reference. Time is no factor except to stay steady and keep momentum.

The prophet Jonah seems to have been a real historical character; however, the narrative is certainly a moral tale devised to make the point of God's mercy and our assurance of universal salvation for all. Though Jonah is not to be imitated, we are to heed his word, even if an anti-prophet gives it. The Ninevites repented and were saved. The prophets were sent to the chosen people of Israel, but not Jonah. He was sent to Nineveh, traditionally known as enemy territory to Israel.

The hearer of this tale would get the plain rendering of the story. Jonah was a reluctant prophet who went the other way instead of responding to God's directive. His ship was caught in a storm and he was thrown overboard by his shipmates to placate the God of the wind and sea. After three days being stored in the belly of a great fish, he was spewed out on dry land—saved. He was again called to deliver the message of God's mercy to Nineveh. He reluctantly went to this city and gave the word to the people and the emperor. To his regret, God repented and changed the plan because all sentient beings of Nineveh repented, even the animals. They put on sackcloth.[1] They changed from their evil ways. All were saved. Jonah was sad rather than glad. He sulked. He rested under a castor oil plant that died just when he needed it most to shield him against the blazing sun. Jonah again blamed God for his misfortune. God rebuked Jonah, saying he failed to get the message that all manner of things are from God; rather, he continued his depressed, self-serving life instead of living toward God and God's will for him.

There is a wonderful prayer in chapter 2. It is written in the literary form of a canticle that is placed on the lips of Jonah, who is in need of God's mercy as he is deep in the sea and deep in the belly of the great fish. The prayer for deliverance seems out of character with the subsequent chapters of the short story, where he continues being a reluctant prophet. The book ends with a tag about saving the twenty thousand people of Nineveh who don't know their left from their right. Saved also are all the animals. This seems to be a humorous way of saying the dumb animals got the message that Jonah missed!

Questions for the Literal Voice

What does the text say? (If my revelatory text is nature or experience I would gather the phenomena in great detail.) Using the example from the book of Jonah, we can ask the following questions.

Who was he? Is he a historical character or a literary device? What is the literary genre of the book of Jonah? Who wrote it? Who is the voice speaking? To whom was it told? Is it one piece or a patchwork of literary texts strung together?

What exactly is the story? Where is the geography it describes? Where are Tarshish and Joppa? Was Nineveh a great city? What is the meaning of giving them forty days to repent? What is a prophet? Was Jonah a prophet? Why did he flee? Who were the crew? What's the call to the Ninevites? Why was Jonah thrown into the sea? Why did the sailors pray to Jonah's God and also offer vows after the sea was calmed? What's the great fish got to do with the story? Why was Jonah so disappointed when the Ninevites repented?

What is that canticle doing in the middle of the sad story? It doesn't fit the actual sequence of the story. The behavior of Jonah changed, but it doesn't seem to be out of gratitude for having his life restored. What is the story saying with all its exaggerations and humor? What is to be understood with the phrase that God changed his mind?

How is this book quoted in the New Testament? What is the context? Who quotes it?

Are there root words or phrases that have particular clues for the literal voice: the name Jonah; running away from God's presence; sleeping under the castor bean plant; watching for the destruction of Nineveh?

Are there variants in translations that provide alternative views of the text's literal voice?

I dig deeply into the text and ask all the questions of the literal voice. I ask the text to reveal itself since I am not the text; it has an integrity of its own. I take the time to write out the whole text. In this case, there are four short chapters, including chapter 2, a canticle that doesn't fit into the sequence of the story. I linger over each sentence and see it as a whole. Other questions arise as I see verse by verse before my eyes.

With my logical mind I do my homework:

- I simply answer those questions in a linear fashion.
- I use my intellect for this mental domain.
- I take my time to steadily and systematically answer question after question.

Answers to Questions of the Literal Voice

Question: Who was Jonah?

Answer: He was a prophet that was a joke, an anti-prophet. Jonah was a prophetic legend, the opposite of the tales such as those told of Elijah and Elisha in 1–2 Kings. A caricature of a prophet told with irony and satire: instead of proclaiming the word of the Lord, he fled and hid his face. The book is sometimes called a parable or a fable. It is a story with a message. Jonah's name means "dove" and has the same root word as Lazarus and Noah.

Question: Is he a historical character or a literary device?

Answer: Most likely Jonah was a fictional literary character even though they used a reference to a real historical descendant of a known tribe. He was an eighth-century prophet from Gath-hepher, a small Galilean town near Nazareth. According to a one-sentence reference in 2 Kings 14:25, there was a prophet in the time of King Jeroboam II (786–46) of Israel called Jonah, the son of Amittai. The name means "trustworthy"!

Question: What is the literary genre of the book of Jonah?

Answer: The book is a spoof full of exaggerated humor. It has an oral literary feel of a tall tale that the audience would have known each detail of when the speaker would recite it time and time again. A parable is a comparison in brilliant story form that seeks to illuminate an issue and, in the process, touches a number of other issues.

Question: Who wrote it?

Answer: It was eventually written down. Though situated in the eighth century BC, this book could have been written down as late as the fifth century BC, contemporary with the books of Ezra and Nehemiah. It is a tight book with literary form that suggests that it was the work of one author. It was a story told and recited word for word by a competent storyteller who had memorized all the details to keep the literary ingenuity.

The author's artistry is evident not only in the obvious symmetry and balance that characterize the book's structure. A number of literary devices serve to knit the episodes in the book more closely together and to enhance the work's subtlety and complexity. These literary techniques include the use of key words such as "great," "evil," "appoint," "fear," and "descend"; not without significance is the way in which the author plays on and exploits the various nuances of these words. His use of exaggeration is comic. The word "great" is used fourteen times.

Question: Who is speaking? Who is telling the story about Jonah? How would this story ever have been known?

Answer: The storyteller must be some Jewish elder. We hear God's voice to Jonah and his response and even inner dialogue, then the dialogue of the sailors on the ship and the report of the great fish. It is told about God, about Jonah, about Nineveh. A prophet tells a story about a non-prophet and reports it to the reader.

Question: To whom is the story directed?

Answer: The readers are many over the centuries: anyone needing the message of universal salvation, about believing that people can change, and that even God can change. God's word is to be trusted, and the hearer does not require major signs to believe and to repent. The prophet is not God, but God can reveal God's loving compassion through anti-prophets who avoid their mission.

Question: Is the story one piece or a patchwork of literary texts strung together?

Answer: The structure has two missions. The first mission includes Jonah and the sailors, his flight, the storm, the great fish. Then comes the second mission: the conversion of Nineveh, the action of the prophet, the reaction of the city, and, finally, God's attempt to convert Jonah. Chapter 2, which reads like a psalm, seems like a later inclusion but is an appropriate sentiment if Jonah had experienced a conversion. It certainly is my sentiment, but this is ahead of the literal voice studied by my logical senses. For this study, I am using my academic training in exegesis that I learned in school.

Question: What exactly is the story?

Answer: Jonah was sent to Nineveh to call them to conversion. The Ninevites would be destroyed in forty days if they did not repent. Jonah went the opposite direction. There was a storm at sea. The seamen prayed to their own gods for salvation. The captain went below to rouse Jonah from sleep and demanded that he pray to his god. The crew cast lots to find out if any passenger was responsible for the storm: Jonah was revealed as the guilty party. Realizing that God had sent the storm because of his disobedience, Jonah begged to be thrown overboard. His wish was reluctantly granted, and, as soon as he was cast into the sea, the storm abated. The Gentile crew offered prayers and homage to the God of the Hebrew people.

Jonah was swallowed by the great fish (*dag gadol*) and after three days and nights was vomited out on dry land (Jonah 2:10). Again, God ordered Jonah to preach in Nineveh. This time he obeyed. The city repented. They put on sackcloth, the traditional symbol of repentance that prophets used to shame erring Israelites. Jonah was infuriated. Instead of being wrathful, God was merciful. God changed from anger to compassion. Jonah was indignant. Jonah slept under shade. The next day the plant withered and Jonah was angry at God for taking away his shade. This part of the story ends with God's message: "You feel sorry for the little plant, yet you did not do any work for it or make it grow. . . . Should I not feel sorry for Nineveh, that great city, in which there are more than twenty thousand people?" (Jonah 4:10-11).

Question: Where is the geography it describes? Where are Tarshish and Joppa?
Answer: Nineveh is modern-day Mozal, Iraq. Joppa is now Jaffa. Tarshish is the tip of Spain. The Jewish annotated

bible signifies that Jonah went to a distant place. We might compare this with my geography in Indiana: Jonah's assignment was to go to Chicago. He went to Alaska and fetched a boat set to pilot around the Florida Keys to get to a port in Maine; then he makes his way to Chicago through the Great Lakes.

Question: Was Nineveh a great city?

Answer: Perhaps Nineveh was considered the region of Assyria; maybe at one time it was a great city. But it seems to fit into the genre of a spoof. At the time of the telling of the story, Nineveh was known to be about the size of a village two blocks by four in area. It would take about an hour maximum to walk from one end to the other, even taking baby steps, or maybe if it took three days we would have to take two steps forward and one step back!

Question: What is the significance of the forty days?

Answer: Seems like the exodus plan that gave passage from Egypt to the chosen people of the Israelites was offered also to the Ninevites. The forty years in the desert was the time it took the chosen people to be converted to the true God and observe the law that was given to Moses. The Ninevites had forty days to turn from their evil ways to abide according to God's compassionate love. The forty years sometimes is referred to in order to expand the testing time beyond one generation. In forty years children grow up and beget children, who might begin to have children of their own.

Question: What is a prophet? Was Jonah a prophet?
Answer: Jonah was a non-prophet. He was self-questioning. He may have been representative of the disillusionment with and disappearance of prophecy that marked this late Old Testament period. Oddly, he may have been a great prophet to turn the audience away from gazing at prophetic messengers and to look only to the One whose messengers they were. The one who is able to achieve God's agenda is sometimes an envoy like Jonah.[2]

Jonah was the only Jewish prophet sent to the Gentiles and not to give the word of the Lord to the Israelites. So the message has a sharp cut that the Gentiles listen and the Jews, even those called to be prophets, do not listen and heed the word of the Lord.

Question: Why did he flee?
Answer: We don't know why. We know that he did refuse to go and went the other way. It seems that Jonah had a disdain for salvation except for those who were the chosen ones of Israel. Nineveh was a wicked city that did not worship the true God, as were the sailors, and the great fish was as big as a whale!

Question: What's the call to the Ninevites?
Answer: This city would be destroyed unless they repented of their wickedness and turned their life around in accordance with the directives of the true God of this oracle.

Question: Why was Jonah thrown into the sea?

Answer: Jonah was disobedient and trying to flee from the assignment. He told the mariners that his God who made the seas was angry with him for his disobedience. The pagans believed in Jonah's God and heeded the warning. When Jonah was thrown overboard along with the cargo, the seas returned to peaceful waters. The storm was replaced by calm abiding. The pagans offered vows and sacrifice to Jonah's God. The pagans were converted to the Lord. Jonah was swallowed by the great fish.

Question: What's the great fish got to do with the story?
Answer: The great fish was a holding place that reversed certain death and gave Jonah a second chance to hear the word of God and act upon it. It is a huge salvation event to deliver Jonah from his flight from God. The great fish as big as a whale is an instrument of God's mercy. Jonah was saved from drowning in the vast and deep sea.[3]

Question: Why was Jonah so disappointed when the Ninevites repented?
Answer: He wanted God to deliver punishment because he thought the Ninevites deserved the consequences of their wicked ways. Jonah wanted only the Israelites saved because they were God's chosen people. There was a double belief for Jonah: His God was the only true God and all other gods were not the One True God. Jonah made the mistaken crossover that since there was only One True God, there was also only One True Chosen People that this God would save. All other gods and all other peoples

were not in the way of salvation. Jonah abstracted the oneness of God and applied the concept to oneness of the chosen people. This limits God and is a wrong assumption of a believer.

Question: What is the canticle doing in the middle of this story? It doesn't fit the actual behavior of Jonah, who was still reluctant even after being rescued.

Answer: The content of the poetic prayer/canticle is all the sentiments Jonah should have had if he had repented. This canticle does what poetry and song can do best: sing through life's troubles and bring us to the other side, like the great fish did in the storyline. Since the Ninevites and the mariners on the ship in the midst of a storm were also saved, they could also have sung this song.

Question: What is the story saying with all its exaggerations and humor?

Answer: The huge swings of the story, the flight, the storm, the whale, the second call from God, the tiny call to the Ninevites who repent on the first day with the king putting on sackcloth and ashes, as well as all the animals who are also fasting. The point seems to be that God is great, that we receive the grace to go God's way, and that we can be assured that mercy will be ours. Universal salvation is God's overwhelming generosity. It is God's judgment, not ours, as to whom he saves and pardons. Our fitting response is repentance. Righteousness is doing the right thing with faith in God's mercy.

Question: What is to be understood by the idea that God changed his mind?

Answer: This is a biblical anthropomorphic metaphor that helps us to understand that our life matters to God. The mind of God responds to our contrite actions.

Question: How is this book quoted in the New Testament? What is the context? Who quotes it?

Answer: The sign of Jonah in Matthew 12:38-42, draws a parallel between the "three days and three nights in the belly of the sea monster" and Christ's three days and nights in the tomb.

Luke 11:29-32 is a challenge to look for signs that reveal rather than keep looking and doubting:

> When the crowds were increasing, he began to say, "This generation is an evil generation; it asks for a sign, but no sign will be given to it except the sign of Jonah. For just as Jonah became a sign to the people of Nineveh, so the Son of Man will be to this generation. . . . The people of Nineveh will rise up at the judgment with this generation and condemn it, because they repented at the proclamation of Jonah, and see, something greater than Jonah is here!" (Luke 11:29-30 and 32)

Question: Are there root words that have particular clues for the literal voice?

Answer: The "running away from God's Presence," "the sleeping under the plant," "watching for the destruction of Nineveh" are images with deep contradictions to awaken the hearer of the story.

Question: Are there variants in translations that provide alternative views of the text's literal voice?
Answer: Yes.[4]

> *NRSV*
> *Oracle:* Go at once to Nineveh, that great city, and cry out against it; for their wickedness has come up before me.
> *Jonah's Response:* But Jonah set out to flee to Tarshish from the presence of the LORD. He went down to Joppa and found a ship going to Tarshish; so he paid his fare and went on board, to go with them to Tarshish, away from the presence of the LORD.
>
> *REB*
> *Oracle:* Go to the great city of Nineveh; go and denounce it, for I am confronted by its wickedness.
> *Jonah's Response:* But to escape from the LORD Jonah set out for Tarshish. He went down to Joppa, where he found a ship bound for Tarshish. He paid the fare and went on board to travel with it to Tarshish out of reach of the LORD.
>
> *NAB*
> *Oracle:* Set out for the great city of Nineveh, and preach against it; their wickedness has come up before me.
> *Jonah's response:* He went down to Joppa, found a ship going up to Tarshish, paid the fare, and went aboard to journey with them to Tarshish, away from the LORD.

NJB

Oracle: Go to Nineveh, the great city, and proclaim to them that their wickedness has forced itself on me.
Jonah's response: Jonah set about running away from Yahweh, and going to Tarshish. He went down to Jaffa and found a ship bound for Tarshish; he paid his fare and boarded it, to go with them to Tarshish, to get away from Yahweh.

So we understand from this little study that, unlike Abraham—who heard the word of the Lord and set out at once to deliver the oracle, got there, and pleaded for mercy on behalf of the wicked city of Sodom, not once, but several times—Jonah simply ignored the directive and fled from the Presence. He hid from God, went away from God, rather than speaking the word of the Lord to Nineveh.

The Logical Senses Receive the Literal Voice

I study this text with my logical senses, continuing over several days. We can understand the text and get at the several layers of literal clues to provide us with a cohesive story to follow. We get its movement from a beginning call, through Jonah's journey, and to the end with a directive from God. We can see him getting on board the ship in Joppa, being thrown in the water, being swallowed by the huge fish, getting thrown up on the shore, and taking baby steps through the town of Nineveh, looking back on the village and being angry that it was changing its way of life even though the inhabitants were Gentiles. We see Jonah totally depleted of energy with depression, sleeping under the cool shade of the plant and then waking in the harsh sunlight. We get the consistent character of his negativity, and we get the humor that Jonah was an anti-prophet who went away from the word of the Lord.

As can be seen, my logical senses can study and study. Commentaries are helpful, but soon I find that commentators disagree with each other and there are ever-new interpretations to consider. Some say the canticle in chapter 2 is a later interpolation. Some say that it is Jonah's truest sentiments from the belly of the whale. The story just shows how quickly we can forget God's mercy and flip back into former ways of life. The point for me in this first phase of *lectio divina* is to do enough homework that I can answer questions about what the text says. Then I need to move on to the next level of working with the text and answering questions about what the text means.

Summary of Literal Reading with Logical Senses

While I may shift into the second dimension of listening with my artistic senses, it doesn't close out the option of doing further referencing and exegetical study. A sign that, for now, I had finished with the literal voice was when I was finding many contradictory explanations about the text. I started reading about the historicity of the text and how Jonah was a real living prophet that literally got swallowed by a fish, and the miracle was that he was not digested. This kind of literalism was taking me off message of a tale of salvation, so I thought it was time to move on to the second dimension of *lectio divina*.

When I'm into the next phase using my more intuitive senses and working with this same text, I might be prompted by grace to come back to this literal-logical work, but with a new question, and start darting around like a weaver or a kneader of dough and not as a scholar proving a particular point of view. Scholarship is invaluable to us as readers of the Bible, but academic investigation has tools and a life of its own. While truth is good in and of itself, and if I am to get beyond the literal level, I must refrain from more study about the text. *Lectio divina* is prayer toward the God mediated through the text.

Some scholars also do *lectio divina*. Academic rigors are beneficial to our faith, but I am free of the endless quest of the literal voice of the text that answers the question, "What does the text say?" *Lectio divina* is more than most Bible study programs, though we might use some of those catechetical materials. We study in the first phase, and then we move on to the meditation and ascetical work of rooting out all patterns that contaminate our hearts. When we repent, like the Ninevites, we can also hear the word of God in our revelatory text. To do this I need to move on from the question of what the text says and ask what the text means. I need to understand the text with my logical mind but then move on to the next level of meaning. The third question is: What does it mean *to me*? But first let me report how I found the meaning of the book of Jonah.

Chapter 3

The Meaning of the Text: The Symbolic Voice Is Grasped by the Intuitive Senses

Teaching on Jonah

At least one of the meanings of the book of Jonah is clearly to proclaim that God is merciful and full of compassion. God's mercy is universal and available to Jews and Gentiles, and full repentance is within the grasp of all who hear the word of God.

The device to get the attention of the reader (or hearer of the story) is humor. Jonah, the reluctant prophet, is pathetic. Instead of going to Nineveh, he went to Africa to get a boat to Spain. The geographical points represent the opposite ends of the earth known at that biblical time.

Jonah was sailing away, and infidels had more faith in his God than he did. When thrown overboard, he was rescued by the foe, a whale, and delivered personally toward Nineveh. When he did get there to deliver his message, he took baby steps through this little town (the people of the time would know that you'd walk it in a couple of hours). It took him a day to get one-third of the way through it, and he whimpered instead of shouted God's directive. Much to his chagrin, everyone repented: the king put on sackcloth, the animals were even draped with shrouds, and all fasted; even the animals were not given food or water. (Now how did they do this?) All repented, the Lord gave mercy in response, and the city was saved. Jonah was not pleased. He sulked, taking a nap under a plant, which withered, causing Jonah to sulk again and complain to God. God rebuked Jonah for his attitude of that only he was to have comfort and mercy.

The meaning of the name Jonah has the same root as Noah, Lazarus, and Dove. Jonah was an antihero who was delightfully instructive and reluctant to do the word of the Lord. The meaning of the narrative is clear: universal salvation is available to all, and God saves us in spite of ourselves. We who believe in God need only to accept God's graciousness.

I grasp the meaning of the story with my intuitive senses and I meditate on the text. I get that the teaching is an instruction on God's love and mercy toward the infidels in the storm who threw Jonah overboard, on Jonah who was unfaithful, on the people and animals of Nineveh, and on the anti-prophet Jonah who was cursing God because his shade was diminished by the sun just doing its job of warming the planet. I certainly get the wonderful canticle of being grateful for being rescued and saved. I use other symbolic vehicles as means to get beneath the story's message, such as music, art, and literature or poetry. I enjoy other tales of total repentance.[1] We learn that the likes of Mary Magdalene, Mary of Egypt, Pelagia, Thais, and Maria the niece of Abraham became confessors not through ordination but through their own authenticity of repentance. The great literary genre of hagiography supplies the way of telling the edifying tale that both inspires and confronts. The strange fact about Jonah is that he never repents. What does this mean?

The Symbolic Voice

What is the meaning of the book of Jonah? This is meditation. I use my artistic senses to gather the whole of this text. I use a different part of my brain: the right hemisphere is usually credited with grasping the meaning behind the symbols. In the Alexandrian tradition this second level has many names: allegorical, christological, typological, symbolic, spiritual, or hidden. The common factor is that words are used to point to something else.

Hidden Meanings

To get at this hidden meaning I used meditation, as in musing or pondering the text. I employed various levels of my inner ways of knowing intuitively.

Listed below is a series of meditations I did with *lectio divina* on the book of Jonah. Notice there is no right starting place and sometimes a repetitive theme comes back for more exploration. I set aside my logical mind. I yield to the intuitive, personal, and spiritual senses that grasp in wholes. Here, in meditation, I can zip and fast-forward to those magical insights that satisfy the intuitive senses. Poetry reigns where algorithms formerly resided.

The symbolic voice gives meaning to the literal voice and does not negate it. It is literally true that the Jews were freed from the slavery of the Egyptians. It is literally true that Jesus rose from the dead. What might not be literal are the symbols used to evoke these truth claims. For example, Jonah might not have been in the belly of a great fish for three days and three nights, but he was rescued from the sea and taken back to his job as a prophet. The literal is in service of the symbolic—the allegorical, typological, symbolic, or hidden voice that speaks of a meaning other than the obvious, literal (plain) message.

Let me be specific. I did various types of meditation on the text. It took me about six months. These types of meditations were all in service of my revelatory text. What makes this *lectio divina*? This is a disciplined approach using my text from Scripture, not a new disclosure from random reading of other interesting books. *This is major*. I linger long and sustain my focus on the book of Jonah. Because I went so deeply into the meaning of the text, it heaved up like my very own storm at sea. It was like a field of flowers springing into life from beneath apparent casual knowledge and my own asphalt-like resistance. Once I realized the teaching from the text, then

I could freely associate not with the biblical text but with the text of my life.

I refrain from keeping my logical senses dominant while I do this meditation process. I refrain from taking the book of Jonah solely as an objectively literal and statistically empirical historical narrative rather than evocative of the deep upon deep mystery. This revelatory text of Scripture points to and is in service of anointing my soul. I respect the symbol of the text and its intended meaning by the author; however, I now meditate for myself. I might find meanings that the author did not foresee. The second level of the aesthetical (symbolic) voice differs from the literal voice because I am still in dialogue with the text as the medium of the encounter and am thinking about the text, but I look at the hidden meanings underneath the text.

This level of commentary and engagement with the literary symbols may dart to similar literature or other media, such as novels or film, but it is all in service of grasping the meaning of our original revelatory text. I become familiar with this second voice that speaks to me in symbol, metaphor, and story. Most of Scripture is to be read like poetry but believed like history. I saw how the shift from medieval exegesis to the historical-critical methods of exegesis caused the literalism of the nineteenth century.

Literalism

The harm done to sincere believers by the ignorance of reading an artistic literary form of scriptural literature as if it were an empirical historical fact continues today. This misguided use of Scripture cannot be dismissed if we are to engage in *lectio divina*. When we engage in the debate of creation done by the Creator God in seven days or if we see this passage to justify the oppression of women since they were created after men, we are misreading the text. It was meant to show that the same God created woman; the man did not create woman. We are reading the symbolic voice with our logical mind (left brain) rather than with our intuitive senses (right brain). The culture that the Bible reflects is parallel to all ancient civilizations that evolved through many phases and stages. Two current uncritical uses of taking the symbolic as a literal fact are still at work in a harmful way in the twenty-first century. Some dismiss Scripture as obsolete, and others try to use the literal voice to shore up moral preferences with sacral legitimating language.

The Church

First, the church is a symbol of Christ's reign on earth. Gregory the Great, who was a monk-pope, used the word "church" for "the Vatican." This was a logical signification of church, as the Vatican was also church, but not the exclusive manifestation of the Christian Church. As the years went on, the literal place dominated Christian consciousness. The shift from the biblical sense of "the Way" to the institution located in Italy not only was an error of reductionism but also drained the reign of Christ of its moral fiber, as taught by St. Paul, and replaced it with canon law. The church is Christ to the extent that it reflects the holiness, compassion, and *kenosis* that Jesus lived while on earth in his historical life. The church is to imitate Jesus.

To the extent that the church misses the mark of institutionalizing the words, deeds, and relationships with all those in need, it is "the church." Abbess Marie Fahy, OCSO, wrote to me recently:

> About the Church—I suppose I simply see it as the Body of Christ through which we are reconciled with God. It is the instrument/means of becoming one with Christ through Baptism/ Eucharist/sacraments. Through the Church we are connected with the early Christian events/people/tradition and remain in communion with the whole Body of Christ, head and members. The Church makes service and love divine intervention in people's lives through our hands.

We need the church, and the church needs a human construct of an institution, but the lofty symbol of "the church" and the function of society are two different meanings of the word "church." The church as proclaimed by St. Paul is the voice received by the intuitive senses. The institution with its pope and staff at the Vatican is a literal voice received by the logical senses. The church imitates Christ, and Christ institutes church to continue his Body in communion with his teachings. This language is using the symbolic voice to give meaning to church. Uncritical assimilation of the culture of the Roman Rite of the Catholic Church is literalism. The

Gospel provides the guide on this earthly side. The Holy Spirit helps us discern the way to be Christian today. The earthly construct of church (as in Vatican, bishops, priests, parishes) is meant to be a visible symbol of the invisible Christ present in our world today.

The "Perfect" State

A second example of reading literally what was originally symbolic is the concept of vocation. The perfect life that St. Bernard rightly praised was his monastic community. It came from his observations of his monks singing the Divine Office with such splendor. Later this concept of the perfect life was read literally rather than figuratively. The hierarchal vocation of the priest or monk being in the perfect state was a literal interpretation of sanctity. There was a leap of logic from the spiritual journey of purgation, illumination, and finally perfection—as in proficient—to simply having taken the vows of a monk or a priest. The call to be a monk or a priest that shifted from these symbolic senses taken literally was unfortunate: it created a caste system putting laypeople on the bottom tier.

This was remedied in theory at Vatican II with the "people of God" being recognized as the church. But the Vatican still has the organizational structures taking this symbolic truth, using a business model of corporate management, and then decreeing that these doctrines and propositions are revelations from God. The two concepts merged: the priest or monk was "the perfect" and the Vatican was "the church."

This indiscriminate cultural assimilation was the result of using the logical senses rather than the intuitive senses to read symbols and myths with their intended meanings. The church is Christ and the institutional Catholic or Orthodox Church is an instrument that Christ uses to mediate revelation, but the human religions are normal sociological institutions that perpetuate bias and overidentification with the group that has all its propensities toward generational sin. The more specific it gets, the more likely that it becomes self-serving and the revelation is not of God.

Tradition taken as a whole is a safer place to put one's faith. Christ is not this pope or this Vatican Curia or this decree. The universal church deserves and gets our respect and assent. We will always need a principle of unity embodied in a pope, a College of Cardinals, an office like the Vatican, but they are human constructs for us to take a wide view of. Jesus said, "I am the way, and the truth, and the life." This early collapse of the symbolic voice read only by the logical senses instead of the intuitive artistic senses has caused much confusion and needless harm.

In summary, there are countless ways literalism can creep into our reading of sacred texts. As Benedictines, we have been aware of this problem from our study of the Rule of Benedict.

The Abbot Represents Christ (RB 2.2)

To uncritically conflate the abbot as Christ is a potentially dangerous hermeneutical situation. This line in the Rule of Benedict is to be read from our intuitive senses, not our logical thinking mind. When Benedict says, "[The abbot] is believed to hold the place of Christ in the monastery,"[2] we understand this to be a strong, true directive about leadership and the singular role of the abbot as superior, but we do not believe that the abbot is Jesus Christ. He acts like Jesus Christ. Also, the abbot himself knows he is not actually Jesus Christ. If the abbot takes this symbolic role as literalism in truth, we would say he is deluded, as in a paranoia psychotic illness. This is the point of reading the voice with the part of the brain that receives the intended meaning of the writer: the literal voice is received by the logical left brain and the symbolic voice is received by the intuitive right brain.

The Intuitive Senses Receive the Symbolic Voice

Medieval exegesis was strong on meditation, reading the Scriptures with the eyes of intuition and artistic appreciation. What were meant to be homilies and commentaries written from the right brain that should have been read as someone's personal intuitive meditations were read with the left brain and taken literally. The scientific, rational, left brain was reading what an artistic right-brain author wrote. The distinctions are major when poetry is taken literally. Biblical literalism has this type of ignorance as its fatal flaw. The genius of the fourfold hermeneutic is that we read each of the voices with senses prepared to receive and interpret the intent of the author.

The insight for me is that, in distinguishing the four voices, I feel I understand the meaning of the content the author intended to communicate. I also feel that this is what St. Benedict had in mind when he directed his monks to do *lectio* four to five hours a day.

Meditations on the Text Itself: The First Level

Below are some ways I meditated on the book of Jonah using my intuitive senses (right brain). These are some of the meditations I did over the course of several months.

Meditation 1: Slow Down

I slowed down reading, slower and slower with attention. I read the text as if I were listening to someone telling me the story aloud.

Meditation 2: Memorize

I memorized the text and repeated it when walking, standing, sitting, before sleep, and on rising. I memorized the canticle of Jonah, that is, Jonah 2:3-11.

Meditation 3: Refrain from Thinking

I sat in silence in the Blessed Sacrament Chapel. I paused often and practiced unthinking. I let thoughts be and refrained from attachment to thoughts, from adding my own commentary. The text had its own dynamic without my input. Slowly, I returned to the text, noticing new meanings. This practice is restful. Read, pause, notice, and read again. It has the feel of savoring yet not consuming. It's close to tasting Scripture and has the feel of its own transmission. Words do not describe it, but when you experience it, you know why Benedict gave monks plenty of time for *lectio*. The practice here is not so much reading and pausing as it is reading and refraining from thinking about anything: simply sit before the text more like you would sit before a picture or icon and enter into the gaze (being seen). Refrain from free-fall thinking by gently bringing the mind back to the Presence.

Meditation 4: Practice Art

During the Beech Grove School of *Lectio Divina*, Sister Juliann set up the art room for the twenty-plus participants. I drew a picture every day from eleven o'clock in the morning until noon. This was a new medium of my text. Color, lines, empty space on the paper took on the character of Jonah and the great fish. The results in just a week were amazing. The object of this art was the doing of the process, not the completed production. Each day, when we ran the weeklong School of *Lectio Divina* retreats, I started over, drawing anew from my meditation on the book of Jonah. It had mostly the feel of water, depth of darkness contrasted with light, and act of being lifted out from the turbulent sea and the jaws of death in the belly of the whale.

Meditation 5: Practice Music

I play songs and chants on Baroque recorders. There is no explicit connection with the book of Jonah, but the practice of music opens my intuitive senses so I can receive the symbolic voice of the text.

Meditation 6: Do Calligraphy

Though visual art is not my gift, I encourage students to write the text in script (calligraphy) and illuminate the beginning letter because I know the actual words of Scripture are a transmission, so it is natural to write them as prayer. I have written in longhand (cursive) the entire book of Jonah or whatever is my sustained *lectio* text. It's pleasing to have the feel of the words passing through my hand.

Meditation 7: Poetry

Jeff Godecker, a priest from the Archdiocese of Indianapolis, sent me a few short verses from his favorite poems he uses to teach poetry as prayer. He says, "I like poems that take me out of myself, open the cage that my ego keeps me in, remind me that I am connected not isolated in self-pity, etc. The image in the two psalms about being in the pit and being taken by God and set down in a broad space is a favorite image conveying the same thing."

Meditation 8: Read Different Editions

I read the text in six translations of the Old Testament. I do not know Aramaic, Hebrew, or Greek. I feel that the multiple translations are an astute way to understand the text. Abbot Laurence O'Keefe of Ramsgate Benedictine

Abbey on the Kent coast (now moved to Chilworth, Surrey) is a brilliant student of Old Testament Hebrew and New Testament Greek. I know of no one who knows the Bible from the heart as he does. I see that even if I were not going to be a Scripture scholar I would have liked to have been given these literary tools for *lectio divina* like the community provided tools for the garden or kitchen.

Meditation 9: Share with a Spiritual Director

I feel that to receive the insights and progress about the revelatory text is the role of a spiritual director. I have never done so until recently. I suppose this is the motive behind writing this book—that is, to help spiritual directors to know what the directee is doing when she shares her revelatory text. The text should be 80 percent of the dialogue with one's formation director, spiritual director, or soul friend. If our appointments default to ordinary conversation, our dialogue tends to go toward problem solving, casual sharing, or just sharing the most recent book or travel. (Those I have in spiritual direction: today I know Matt is doing Jeremiah and the broken cistern, Julie is doing repentance *lectio* from the book of life, Ed is doing *Story of a Soul* from Thérèse, Jim is doing an encounter with Jesus in the gospels, etc.)

Meditation 10: Form Space

I keep in my cell a space for my *lectio*. I have the book out and marked at the place of my next session. Another practice of my cell is to keep it uncluttered so that the *lectio* work is first priority in space and time. I take care to form the space so that the space will form me.

Meditation 11: Text as Prism

I hold the text in my heart, on my mind, and in my mind's eye as I filter in and out the usual daily thoughts. The text becomes a prism or my most recent template. I need some Jonah time, away from all that I think I'm doing. Or, I feel in need of repentance. What would be a contemporary form of sackcloth and ashes?

Meditation 12: Encounters

After some months of living into the text, the meaning seems to grow beyond the book. I see references everywhere. I like to photograph community events. Looking through the lens of life, like looking through the camera's viewfinder, I see aspects of the Jonah story slicing in and out of my reality: nuns we thought were in a dying condition suddenly get better and are at table the next day. Or there is more zeal living a simple life in an oblate (the Gentiles) than in the fully professed nuns (Israel). Or the playful themes of the current meditation dance around in the scenes of nature and the usual encounters with people during the day.

I've even seen some of the images from the book of Jonah in my dreams. At odd times during table conversations, phone calls, even e-mails I catch insights that recall the text or the meaning of the text in another medium. Ordinary awareness has a way of expanding so the new realizations fit nicely. When I make a week of retreat, I take the last three days as if I were in the whale. I go down, deep as I can go. I practice stillness, close my eyes to all the new stimuli. I stay there without analysis or commentary. I'm in that belly, in that whale, waiting upon salvation. There is nothing I can do. Notice that to describe this I use images and symbols. When I actually do this three-day meditation, it cannot be described in linear logical words.

Meditation 13: From Light to Light

Sometimes, like a daydream, I get an idea-to-idea, feeling-to-feeling that shifts mediums of sensory input. Literally, I can go from light to light until insight rises. One such meditation was how resistant Jonah was to salvation of the Gentiles. This issue on universal salvation is a thorny topic today. I wrote a primer for Catholics about Islam. I continue to get mail that warns me that my Muslim friends will not be saved. At core, the argument of my challengers is that they do not think Muslims are entitled to respect because they are in error. There is still a belief that there is no salvation outside of the Catholic Church and that other faith traditions are not revelations from the same God. This self-righteousness was Jonah's error.

But through my meditation on the universal salvation theme I have experienced the reality of the teachings! We all worship the same God. This not only makes us brothers and sisters relating together on the same planet Earth but also places us with our faces to the ground, worshiping the same God. The insight here is that we are not only universally saved but also universally related as brothers and sisters. So my meditation is not about the Jews of old and their pagan neighbors but about who lives in Nineveh today. Where am I being sent? What's God's word that God wants heard, first by me and then by others?

Meditation 14: Subtle

Running from the Lord can be subtle and we don't notice that we are doing it. My missing the Lord's directives and going the other way may not be as dramatic as Jonah: for example, it might mean taking a vacation for a little while from vigilance, or thinking, "Just not now, next time," or, "Maybe I take this too seriously." Running from the Lord is jerking away from the graces received. This is the heart of the spiritual journey: to accept and heed the word of the Lord.

Meditation 15: Christ in the Scriptures

Read Christ back through Scripture. Augustine and other fathers did this especially in their homilies.[3] While this is Christocentric, my training in East–West dialogue helped me to be sensitive to our Jewish brothers and sisters by realizing that the Hebrew Scriptures stand alone as a revelatory text and that God speaks through them. Salvation comes to all in separate and distinct ways. Yet to read Christ back into the Hebrew Bible is exactly what the early church did and also brought forward in our liturgical texts. So I have no agenda to convert my contemporary Jewish brothers and sisters, but part of my Judeo-Christian heritage is to do that work of study back into the first covenant: I go back and forth, seeing that Jesus is the Messiah, the New Law, the New Covenant, the New Moses, and the Lord of Jerusalem.

The four voices of Scripture are a tool to separate the literal from the symbolic. Jerusalem is a city in Israel. Jerusalem is God's dwelling. Going up to Jerusalem is to live righteously, keeping faithful to the law day and night and praying ceaselessly. Jerusalem is where we are headed in the next life. As much as God's reign is "now" through Christ Jesus, Jerusalem, the symbol of God's reign, is at work in my here and now. Then comes a meditation of how Jesus says that a greater prophet than Jonah is in our midst. God's work is living, conscious, and active.

Meditation 16: Holy Spirit Is Guide

I read some other books that my Jonah *lectio* prompted: for example, *The Prophet* by Abraham Heschel or *The Book of Isaiah* (Anchor Bible). The Holy Spirit is my guide as to what further reading is helpful. By myself I tend to drift from one book to the other.[4] I used to read a book cover to cover no matter if halfway through it I felt it was a dead end. Now, I pick up and read but only as much and as long as I feel the text is moving me toward the theme of my *lectio*. If I do casual reading, I don't play games that it is "for the sake of my soul," so I am truthful to myself. With my recent eye problems, I don't waste eye power on much other than my *lectio*, so that condition actually has served my soul well! Again, like Jonah, I have not been able to avoid the word of the Lord!

In summary, this meditation phase takes time. It needs lots of soft time. This is not something academic that ever has a deadline. Nor is it functional, as preparation for a homily or for lesson plans for teaching. This sinking-in kind of *lectio* is like a spring rain. The trick is to stay on message, that is, to stay with my revelatory text and refrain from getting sidetracked into a new piece of music, pottery, or artwork that expresses my artistic talent but would be an obstacle toward my revelatory text. It is important to select those art forms that are in service of the God encounter as revealed in the event of *lectio divina*.

The functional benefit of doing *lectio* does return through the back door, though. If we do *lectio divina* to the core and if our habitual afflictions that cause us to resist the word of the Lord are rooted out (as we'll see in the next chapter), we can trust that our *lectio* is in service of our ministry. This is tricky because if we "use" *lectio*, we never find that burning bush that gives us the authority to preach and teach. The process of doing *lectio* as a sustained and deep practice is to shift into that realm where God is in us. But this is ahead of my story in chapter 4.

It seems to me that in my early years of doing *lectio*, just when it was going deep enough to effect conversion, I slid off the text and went back into superficial reading. The practice of spiritual reading for me was harmful. I just read book after book. The content stayed in my head and the sheer amount of text tended to keep me far from taking action, as in heeding the directive coming from the text. I read like an observer, not like a participant. I was in dialogue with the author or with the text but not with God, as in a revelatory text.

I feel that the role of the spiritual director is to keep the practitioner on his or her event of God encounter through *lectio divina*. This is very difficult for both the director and the directee: the director must do this *lectio divina* to have the experience to know what the directee is talking about and the directee needs to do it long enough to have some experience to share.

The tradition provides us with much light, but the teachers must know it by doing it. Then, together as a faith community, we can teach it with confidence. As in all practices, unless one is a practitioner there is no inner grasping from experience. *Lectio divina* cannot be comprehended from the outside.

How do I know it has completed its work? When is it time to move toward another revelatory text?

At some point (not of our choosing) we observe another text rising and taking center position in our consciousness. It feels like a Mozart symphony when the point—and then counterpoint—rises and takes over as the dominant theme. There's a brief dissonance as they pass by one another but also a deeply satisfying resolution when the harmonics balance and play off each other. At first, one theme is on top, then the other; a version of the first wiggles through, then diminishes, and the new theme becomes the center voice.

Now I want to return to the book of Jonah and show a few examples of meditation done directly on the text that carries its message.

Meditations on the Meaning of the Text: The Second Level

Meditation 1: Symbols Stored in the Actual Text

The concentric structure of the scenes within scenes is like a modern art film: instead of going up to Nineveh, Jonah goes down to Tarshish, then down to Joppa, down into a ship, down into its hold, and, finally, down to the bottom of the sea and into the belly of a great fish. The countermovement is the sailors' fear of the storm, which becomes a great fear and then a religious fear (awe). Then when they are delivered from danger, they acknowledge the God of Israel while Jonah affirms belief in the God "who made the sea and the dry land" while he drowns in the sea. The storm is calmed, the pagan crew is saved, and they confess faith in and offer vows and submission to the true God. So while Jonah goes down the pagans go up. This movement is repeated with the Ninevites' conversion and the castor oil plant.

Meditation 2: References to Other Passages in Scripture

The voice that comes from great literature such as this is no accident and is the work of a master artist using every word in the text for our instruction.

There are at least twenty words in the text that use a symbol to evoke meaning: "three days and three nights," "the great fish," "the wind," "each cried to his god," "fear," "for they knew," "Jonah sets out," "one day's journey."

The word "oracle" in Hebrew is used only five times in the Old Testament. Jonah's oracle has only five words in Hebrew that have parallels: in Genesis 18:21; 18:22-23; 19:13; 19:25. What is an oracle? A source of wisdom; someone or something considered a source of knowledge, wisdom, or prophecy. It's a wise saying, a wise or prophetic statement.

The listeners of the oral telling of the book of Jonah would have known these oracles: Jeremiah 18:7-10; Exodus 34:6-7; Numbers 14:18; Nehemiah 9:17; Psalms 86:15; 103:8; 145:8; Joel 2:13.

To meditate on an oracle took me to looking for that kind of "word of the Lord" in our times. It seems like there is a refreshing oracle-like theme blowing in my circles of friends. I'll name three oracle-like directives: (1) don't teach beyond your practice; (2) silence is worth the trouble to do whatever it takes to get some; (3) we are all in this boat together.

Meditation 3: Universal Salvation

Jonah 1:16 says, "Then the men feared the LORD even more, and they offered a sacrifice to the LORD and made vows."

One of the wonderful teachings of the book of Jonah is this revelation of universal salvation. All come to God through many, many doors, but there is a pattern of bowing in reverence, lifting up our hearts and minds in prayer, and then ratifying our good zeal with sacrifice. I find that my life is full of bowing and prayer but short on sacrifice—and even shorter on offering gratitude for favors received.

I lingered with these following passages from the Psalms: "Offer to God a sacrifice of thanksgiving, and pay your vows to the Most High" (50:14); "So I will always sing praises to your name, as I pay my vows day after day" (61:8); "Praise is due to you, O God, in Zion; and to you shall vows be performed" (65:1); "My vows to you I must perform, O God; I will render thank-offerings to you. For you have delivered my soul from death, and my feet from falling, so that I may walk before God in the light of life" (56:12-13). In the King James Version, this is translated, "For thou hast delivered my soul from death: wilt not thou deliver my feet from falling, that I may walk before God in the light of the living?" (56:13).

Meditation 4: Conversion

"And the people of Nineveh believed God; they proclaimed a fast, and everyone, great and small, put on sackcloth" (Jonah 3:5).

What signs of conversion would I offer today?

- Express regret
- Go to confession
- Publicly apologize

- Ritualize change of heart
- Do moderate fasting
- Refrain from one little comfort for the sake of renouncing my former way of life
- Do apostolic service instead of personal gain

Meditation 5: God Cares

"When God saw what they did, how they turned from their evil ways, God changed his mind about the calamity that he had said he would bring upon them; and he did not do it" (Jonah 3:10). There are several Old Testament and New Testament examples where asking actually mitigates the outcome: we repent, but also God changes. This is a wonderful exchange. It takes faith in God and in our power of prayer.

Meditation 6: References

Psalms 86:6; 31:22; 34:6; 31:6; and 50:14, according to the Holman Christian Standard Bible, a Protestant translation, have the same theme as the canticle in the book of Jonah. Concerning the psalms that are the same theme but cited as parallels in the New Jerusalem Bible—Psalms 120:1; 130:1; 116:3; 42:7; 31:22; 5:7; 69:1; 30:3; 16:10; 22:25; 116:18; 3:8; 86; Lamentations 3:55—notice that the differences of psalm citations between Catholic and Protestant translations are more than the numbering systems: different psalms are listed.

Other Scriptures that could be referenced are 1 Kings 8:38; 2 Kings 17:15; Hosea 14:2.

The canticle in the book of Jonah is a mosaic of psalm texts and is constructed on the conventional pattern of thanksgiving psalms: description of sufferings undergone and an account of deliverance from them. For the psalmists, grave danger is "death" and deliverance is a "resurrection" (cf. here verses 6-8). The sea, God's primordial "enemy" (cf. Job 7:12ff.) is seen either as the kingdom of death itself or at least as the way that leads to it. Hence, we have the dramatic expressions of this song which enables Jesus (Matt 12:40; Luke 11:30) to use the episode of Jonah as a figure of his own three-day stay "in the heart of the earth" (Sheol, rather than the tomb; cf. Jonah 2:2-3). The kingdom of death is depicted as a greedy monster that cannot hold Christ but must let him go (the resurrection). The analogy between Christian baptism and the resurrection of Christ has led to the use of the figure of Jonah in baptismal typology.

Meditation 7: True Piety

Martin Buber has termed, in a memorable phrase, "the religion of pure psychic immanence."[5] There is a tendency among my generation to collapse on God, which is true piety. But then, if there is not the accompaniment of the willingness to repent and change our lives, we risk making our experience of ourselves God, instead of meeting the true Holy One who is our Creator and transcends our realm. The moral voice cannot be heard if we are supersaturated with our self-made thoughts. We encounter God in *lectio divina*.

The second dimension of knowing our text through listening to the symbolic voice with our intuitive senses takes discipline and ample leisure time. This is the work of the monastery to take long, lingering, loving attention to our revelatory text.

In the next chapter we will take an extended look at the moral voice of our revelatory text. When we listen with our personal senses, we hear that prophetic action required on our part. At first it is usually our own afflictions that need attention, but the good news is that there are many ways to shift our selfishness to selflessness and hear the word of God in our hearts.

Chapter 4

The Moral Voice: Heard and Heeded by the Personal Senses

The Third Dimension

The desert elders memorized the Scriptures and prayed without ceasing. They pondered through the duration of vigils and manual labor. The word was not only heard but also heeded. To engage in study and meditation is only half of the prayer we call *lectio divina*. This essential doing of the word shifts the mind to the heart, and we hear the call as a personal invitation to doing something about the word that is heard. Without the personal response the word remains a dead letter of the law. It's been said to the Cistercian formation directors that the longest journey is not from birth to death but from the mind to the heart.

With the personal response, we walk in the privileged garden of intimacy with the Lord like our ancestors did before our times. It is not until this third dimension is activated that *lectio divina* becomes prayer: it becomes a living, conscious, active way of being before God. We know God. From our side this is deeply personal, as in a relationship. Before it might have been *about* God or *about* us, but this personal voice is *to* us and we lift up our hearts and minds *to* God. This personal response might be in three simultaneous senses: first, we humbly repent, remove obstacles to our relationship; or second, we might pray from our heart and soul; or third, we simply do the word, as in charity and personal outreach toward the poor.

Again, let me review that *lectio divina* has four dimensions, the four voices received by the four senses. In the first dimension I studied what the text of the book of Jonah said. In the second dimension I asked what the book of Jonah means. In this third dimension I ask the question, "What does the book of Jonah mean *for me*?" What is it asking of me? What is my personal response? The fourth dimension will be a separate chapter, but it answers the question of the encounter with God. It is an experience of God beyond the text but revealed through the text.

What Does the Text Mean to Me?

It is after this third dimension—which takes a lifetime—that the mystical voice rises and that my spiritual senses are mature enough to receive those subtle stirrings with the ear of my heart. Periodically, this happens, but I do not seem to be able to sustain a life of continuous attention to the Presence. Time and time again I lift up my heart toward God. Soon, and very soon, I realize I cannot sustain my good intentions. I have so many distractions. My mind seems weak. I get vaguely confused about what I had started to do in my prayer life. I become unfocused and fragmented.

My personal response to the word is a call to the ascetical life. The ascetical life is to undergo purgation, to purify my mind. In all great religions believers must renounce their former way of life and accept the consequences of the revelation. Renunciation is not optional because my choices must line up toward God's call rather than continue the path toward self and maybe even toward evil. This is my vocation, to follow my calling from God.

I have work to do that will help me to respond to God's invitation to me. This personal work depends on grace, but we have the duty to respond with right effort, a humble willingness to do whatever is necessary to follow the directives of the Holy Spirit. We return to our *lectio divina.*

More than enjoying an edifying tale, I can hear the Jonah story and see that it is not directed back in history to the Ninevites but talking to me. I can even hear the directive from the revelatory text but fail to respond. Sometimes my heart simply feels hard and not available even to myself, let alone to some outside source. So what do I do with the book of Jonah?

I do not want to be like Jonah, but I see my same patterns in his story. I want to change, repent, and make my vows to the Lord. I can now close the book. This inner work is my responsibility. I can no longer simply meditate out there about somebody else. I am everyone in the story. I again invoke the Holy Spirit to help me shift from thinking to meditating and observing my thoughts. This prepares me for praying to God. The revelatory text now has done its thing and I must do my work. This is the heart of *lectio divina*—to face God's directives. This is my encounter with the living God. This voice can sometimes be fierce or meek. This is the burning bush. It scorches and transforms.

Obstacles

I know it is difficult to keep at work doing my *lectio* in the midst of our contemporary noise. The world does its own sustained *lectio*. It is called a secular culture that has its own burning acid of influence: shopping at the mall with its music, patterns of display, scripted conversations, eating, and shopping. Even gas stations have piped loud music and advertising outdoors. The mind of our culture is the media; the media is controlling our culture. We, the consumers, are perpetuating this culture with our secular way of life. Much of it is good, not to be negated, but much of it is also a good that is not God.

Even in the monastery I find us continuously listening to the news on the television or radio, reading the daily paper, keeping up with the online versions of the news, or listening to the many commentators. We are immersed in the current events. We are doing with the news what tradition invites us to do with *lectio*. The content can be sports, politics, economy, or news of natural disasters. We are immersed in electronic devices. It took me a few years to tame my electronics, to use technology in service of my *lectio* rather than a culture of the world.[1]

This third dimension of *lectio* is to shut the book. I am ready to act. I ask God, "What would you have me to do?" The trick is to refrain from returning to my former way of life that I did before I have heard and heeded the word of the Lord.

This is difficult to describe and can only be learned by actually doing the wisdom of the first two levels of the *lectio*. But if this step is skipped, then the *lectio* will remain about someone else or one more conceptual abstraction that soon becomes inert. This is also what is meant by "sustained *lectio*." This goes deep and takes on a life of its own. In fact, this life under the river, as it were, is the culture of the monastery.

Can I receive a transmission of grace from the revelatory text? Can I actually feel that I am in need of God's mercy? I need the amazing ability both to repent, as in the case of the Ninevites, and to have a surge of grace to root out the causes and sources of my sin. I see the quick response on the part of the king of Nineveh. What is more important about this third sense is that I shift out of the story and into my own story—my need for being rescued and to realize that I have indeed been rescued. I see the canticle as my story and I pray to have the strength to repent and change course. I might need a downtime of reorientation as in the belly of the great fish. I might need to replace my harsh judgment of others with my own recognition that I'm the one that needs to change. I know I need this ongoing ceaseless repentance.

This third sense is active and personal. The story is not about someone else; it's about me or, collectively, us, but I start with myself. I have agency. I need to act selflessly and without return. I hold on to the word of God as a personal promise and participate in its efficacy.

There is no longer a place to hide. I need grace and guts. I now feel the stirring from underneath. I have never experienced the trembling felt by some ecstatic brothers and sisters, but over and over again I've hit the wall of no return. From the tradition I can list four stages to undergo to receive and follow this directive of the moral voice:

1. I pray directly to God (*oratio*).
2. Yet I cannot sustain this attention toward God because of my sinful tendencies. My sinful tendencies are diminished through ascetical work of renunciation.
3. These propensities toward sin and selfishness are replaced with ceaseless prayer.[2] Where once there was a constant attraction to one of the eight desires that can become passions that would be sinful (food can be gluttony, sex can be lust, things can be

greed, anger can be rage and even murder, dejection becomes depression that could end in suicide, *acedia* can take me off the spiritual journey and give up God, vainglory can make me want to be my own God, and pride can harm myself and others in the name of the god that is me), there can be a fierce desire for God that shifts me away from myself.

4. In abiding in Christ's presence I hear the still, soft, and gentle voice of the Holy Spirit directing my choices. This is called discernment. Spiritual direction helps us with this important personal guidance system.

First, I see that my greatest obstacle to hearing the word and heeding it is my afflictions. The word "affliction" is code for one of the sinful patterns of thoughts listed above that has come down in tradition as the seven capital sins. Two afflictions in particular seem to cover me again and again: anger leading to depression and vainglory enslaving my affect in service of ego rather than honor and glory to God.

Second, I know God loves me very much and I love God, but my weakness is thick; the human condition, in which I live, puts me at risk. I always need to find that window of freedom of choice. What is hardwired in me because of my human genome map? What is my conditioning from being born into the Funk family from Indiana? What is my personal sin that is mine to bear—both consequences and tendencies?

I don't want to be like Jonah, but I do want to be like the Ninevites. I must repent of past sins. The rite of confession or sacrament of reconciliation is my usual starting point. On the retreats here at Beech Grove we like to offer the opportunity of confession on Tuesday night so that the rest of the week we can move into a life of prayer practices.[3] We teach that there are three kinds of confessions: (a) a general confession that reports the sins of a lifetime, (b) a confession reporting sins since one's last confession, and (c) a devotional confession that reports one or two areas of sinfulness that need divine assistance toward conversion.

There is a fourth kind that is rarely used but that I have found to be quite helpful. It is to use confession to beg for mercy in an "area of need." For example, before I started writing the book *Humility Matters*, I went to confession and confessed my need for humility even to dare writing such a book. Before writing this book on *lectio divina* I went to confession and asked for a blessing on this manuscript. Before writing *Discernment Matters*, I confessed my sins, asking for forgiveness of all my indiscretions of a lifetime. The point here is that the moral voice cannot be heard by my personal senses if I am blinded by sin. Personal sins cover the mind and take away purity that sees clearly God's way rather than my self-centered ways.

Training the Mind

The person, now reconciled with God, embarks on a program of training the mind to prevent repetition of sin and to root out sinful inclinations. This training, in part, is to guard one's heart and to watch one's thoughts.

Guard of the Heart

Guard of the heart is to prevent easy entrance into one's heart thoughts of the persons, places, and things that take one away from God. This is an opportunity to change one's habits of conversation, reading, television watching, interaction with others who have similar compulsions or addictions (food, entertainment, drugs or alcohol, relationships, excessive use of things, and excessive amounts of things to do), all of which dulls one's senses. Fatigue causes laxity of willingness to stay faithful to one's inner disciplines. So the *practice* is to avoid temptation. To foster purity of heart we practice staying in places that do not endanger our souls. The *praxis* is to descend our mind into our heart and live from inside our body/mind and soul. But this gets ahead of our teaching.

Watchfulness of Thoughts

To watch our thoughts is not only to notice the content of thoughts that loop around and ultimately cause unwanted actions but also to watch the stage of the thought and catch it early and often and anticipate its rising.

Keeping vigil serves to offset with attention what formerly was working on the mind unconsciously. If we are vigilant, we anticipate situations or catch the first inkling of thoughts that get us into trouble. The person learns to notice afflictions rising, no matter what the content (food, sex, things, anger, dejection, *acedia*, vainglory, and pride).

The person gently but quickly uses the practices that turn gently toward the five antidotes that help us to root out the afflictions:

1. Pray without ceasing using a mantra.[4]
2. At the first instance of temptation, pray an arrow prayer like, "O God, come to my assistance. O Lord, make haste to help me."
3. Shift one's attention from the afflictive thought or emotion toward selfless service or another prayer practice: for example, the Little Way, or practice of recollection.
4. Remember one's death.
5. Combat the affliction with a quote from Scripture.

The watching of thoughts presumes we know the teachings about thoughts: we keep our attention to watch how these thoughts rise, and we use one of the antidotes to refrain from being engaged with the thought and consenting to its invitation.

Here's how the thought works:

1. The thought rises.

2. An image appears.
3. The dialogue of my mind starts up and is accompanied by an image.
4. This evolves into an invitation (a) to continue the dialogue or (b) to refrain from the same.
5. I consent to the inner promptings of further imaging and conversation inside my head accompanied by feelings.
6. The thought gets solid and offers a suggestion to take action.
7. I either take action or refrain from the invitation/ temptation.
8. There's a simultaneous melody line that is another conversation with the thought and the person in this thinking mode about intention/motivation; tradition calls this the "second thought."
9. I act on the invitation one time.
10. I continue in that direction of the original prompting (an affliction).
11. I continue being engaged with that thought that is now an entity accompanied by emotion (passion).
12. I act often in collaboration with the passionate emotion and it becomes a habit (pattern).
13. I then dwell in that ethos of suffering (*pathos*) until
14. this entity, the spirit of the passion, becomes my identity (captivity).
15. I am the thought!

To anticipate our tendencies, we keep vigil rather than become a victim of our weaknesses. This is the purpose of the first Divine Hour of Office in the wee hours of the morning: to rise before the thought (the sun) that shines in our heart and takes us away from our one desire to seek God. We recite the psalms that are similar hopes, dreams, and afflictions of those who went before us.

This third dimension of *lectio divina* is prayer by virtue of intention. Removing our rust (traditional word for sin) is the purgative way that takes most of our lifetime. There are many stories in antiquity of being surprised at an unlearned monastic who has more insights into Scripture than a learned scholar. The practitioner who has moved through to the other side of the afflictions enjoys purity of heart. With purity of heart one can read and hear the revelatory text without hindrance.

This training of the mind is more than backing out the afflictions: this is also the positive work to train the mind to cultivate a Christ consciousness. Prayer replaces a food consciousness, sex consciousness, thing consciousness, anger consciousness, etc. Prayer cultivates an abiding consciousness of God's presence in a spirit of humility.

You might be asking, "What does this training have to do with my revelatory text that I am using for *lectio divina*?" It has everything to do with prayer, and *lectio divina* is a prayer. We cannot expect to lift our heart to God in prayer if we do not use the right effort to rid ourselves of all that is not God. You might still be asking about your text, "Wouldn't studying and meditating on my text also purify my heart and provide purity of heart so that I can relate to God with my desires?" The answer is that we must make the effort to repent and change our lives. Intentions make it easier, but we must also with God's grace follow through with actions that demonstrate and actualize our ongoing conversion. We can never rule out the possibility of a God encounter at any time and any place, but because of our human condition we simply cannot "will it" and expect prayer to sustain us. In a spirit of humility, we must do our own ascetical work. Again, if *lectio divina* is prayer and the third dimension is to do the dynamic moral action required to do the word, we must do the inner work to remove obstacles so that prayer can spring up.

Besides the fact we cannot just "will it" and sustain our conversion, we also have the darkened mind consequence of primordial sin. I can hear a teaching, a wonderful homily, or a compelling presentation on the gospels or monastic discipline. Hearing the truth seldom has the power to help me do it. It seems we must do the word through rigorous and steady practice.

Thomas Hopko, an Orthodox teacher, speaks of the three types of sin.[5] Primordial sin is the brokenness of our human condition of our culture because of hundreds of years of sinfulness. Generational sin includes the sin of five to seven immediate generations before I was born. My historical life is saturated with much of those same tendencies toward selfishness and sin. Some tendencies are so thoroughly ingrained as to have altered chemistry. The

Orthodox teaching, then, is that mood disorders, same-sex orientation, or addictions, for example, are habits formed generation after generation, causing genetic shifts that an individual cannot reverse. In other words, such tendencies are not willful personal choices but characteristics found in our genetic makeup. Finally, there is personal sin that is made of my own sinful patterns that are ever ready to constellate again and become actions and habits. The three types of sin highlight the fact that individuals have a small window of free choice, but it is that freedom and grace that makes all the difference. We will be judged on that little percent left over from our human condition of sin. The good news is that we are not personally guilty of all the rest, but we do our little part to strive against the currents that carry one away from God and goodness.

The word "sin" is controversial. It gets confused with self-centered guilt and self-righteous judgment. We have no better word for the effect of our full consent to doing evil rather than good when we had the possibility. This teaching clearly demonstrates that primordial and generational sin have their personal consequences for each of us but that it is only personal sin that we need to confess and repent. This personal appropriate guilt can be both omission or commission of social sin or particular sin that has been my doing. Yet we know that in this whole entanglement with the human condition we can count on God's mercy.

In the practice of *lectio divina*, we strive to *do* the word that is revealed to us. If we do not do the word, we also do not know the word. This doing the word also has several layers. It takes a lifetime to learn through this doing of the monastic or contemplative way of life (this life under the river). This inner-life activity starts with retraining the mind to make choices consciously rather than live the routine of our former way of life unconsciously (my life as seen by others above the river).

Once I asked my Hindu teacher why I was not feeling any benefit from my years of meditation practice. She said that my life was not in order. I was being quite diligent about my thoughts during actual sitting for meditation, but during the day, as in ordinary consciousness, my mind was in free fall. My actions were not consonant with my monastic way of life. I was out of balance in this third dimension of my moral life. I was not immoral but not morally acting into my vow of *conversatio morum* (ongoing conversion). As Catholic and Orthodox Christians, we are able to detect gross sin and quickly repent, but our Christian traditions lack training of the mind to keep our thoughts in harmony with our ceaseless prayer. Training of the mind prevents sin.

I found that the Christian teachings in the early monastic fathers and mothers of the desert could teach me how to discipline my mind and body. To my delight, they were the same sources that Benedict used for his Rule. I was a vowed nun in the sturdiest tradition that trains the mind to live the moral life but did not know it and did not practice this interior discipline.

Benedict would presume that we did this third dimension of heeding the moral voice with our personal senses.

This is not another practice. This is *lectio divina*; the core of doing the word follows the listening to God's word.

This third dimension of *lectio divina* is to hear the moral voice that calls us to action. The action is both to refrain from selfishness and sin and to cultivate a Christ consciousness so that prayer replaces all the self-talk and interior passivity. The interior life requires strenuous effort. We are attentive to our thoughts and guard against free-falling thoughts that become temptations and actual deeds that take us away from God. We replace our mindlessness with mindfulness and take up the training of ceaseless prayer practices.

Observance/Practice/*Praxis*

Another difficulty to sustaining *lectio divina* is to be deprived of a faith community. We need church. We need the sacraments of baptism, reconciliation, and Eucharist. We need priests and a well-ordered society that can be provided by a well-ordered organization called church. New forms of church are emerging, and new forms of religious life are rising rapidly, but in the meantime, we need nourishment now. Membership in a local church is not optional. As broken as systems can be, we still need the services they provide. We can be more effective from within than from without. Remaining at table is challenging but can be done—and done well with our inner practices giving us the inner directives we can trust. Jonah was not called to start his own Israel but to give the word of the Lord to the neighbors. We all need the support of others, and others as an intentional group. Our church needs a new pentecost today where we gather and are quickened by the Holy Spirit, where that inner law planted in our hearts can find like-minded souls to be church together, reach out to the poor, and replicate the words and deeds of Jesus.

Three Degrees of Inner Work

Monastics have this support. We observe the Rule together. When one comes into a monastery it should be easy to see the life in common with shared things, common table, and worship in the assembly. The schedule (*horarium*) is a requirement of membership to be taken seriously. Permission is necessary if one is to be absent. More important than observance is practice. Each of the observances requires a particular discipline. This inner work is the work of the monastery. The training is for group practices to protect the solitude that is conducive to do this inner work.

When one comes to the monastery, the cloister, or the retreat house, one enters into the practice of silence. The setting provides the solitude that protects and gives boundaries to the practice of silence. Within the practice of silence, we discipline the thoughts of the mind (*praxis*). This *praxis* is about our thoughts: what we are doing with our minds while we practice silence in the observance of solitude. These three concentric degrees of inner work is the work of the monastery. We specialize in this inner life, the spiritual journey.

So there are three concentric circles or degrees of work for the sake of this contemplative life:

1. Observance is what people see and is something done for the sake of the silence.
2. Practice is the inner discipline done within the observance.
3. *Praxis* is the training of the mind that we do while we are doing the practice within the observance.

Examples: Silence and Statio

In the cloister we "observe" silence. This ritual is seen by others. Within this observance is the "practice" of silence: we set aside designated times, places, and degrees of restrictions to honor the solitude. And within the practice of silence is the *praxis* of stillness. *Praxis* is what one does with one's mind that governs thoughts and emotions. *Praxis* would be stillness of mind and body. Both the mind and the body require discipline of thoughts. Thoughts matter! The digital consciousness of where to direct the mind's eye stills the stream of mental images and the ever-shifting movements of the body. Sensations are noticed but not heeded, both in the mind and in the body. When guests come to a retreat at Beech Grove, we request compliance with the norms of silence in the solitude of the monastery. Then we give training on how to still the mind and emotions as well as how to still the body (*praxis*).

Another such example of observance, practice, and *praxis* is *statio*. We stand outside of the church and line up, maintaining silence (observance that one can see from the outside). Before processing into church for Vespers we listen to the tolling bells (practice of place, ritualized gestures in actual time). With our mind, we practice recollection, reining in all our senses and bringing our thoughts to stillness, emptiness (*praxis*). With each toll of the bell, we ride out the thoughts to come to that place of the present moment when we are ready to enter the temple of worship.

The teaching on practice and *praxis* is important for this third dimension of *lectio divina* because just inserting ourselves into the observances of the contemplative culture won't save us. We must train our mind to enter into the practices with assiduous *praxis*. *Lectio divina* is an encounter with God but first we must wake up and encounter ourselves and redirect our thoughts away from self and toward God's way for us.

These three concentric circles work from outer to inner, conversely. Without the outer observance, there is no structure to protect the practice. The practice is the connecting tissue to provide matter for the mind. *Praxis* without the practice would be nominal, or simply mind-only manipulations that tend to reify reality. We think things exist and so they do. So we need all three: *praxis*, practice, observance, or we can start with observance, practice, and *praxis*. The embodiment of these three solid traditional means of contemplative life is the monastic way of life. This is not to say that lay life cannot be contemplative, but it does raise the serious question about structures to steady the practice and give form so the *praxis* becomes a habit. The culture of the world often opposes this inner work of prayer.

The method for both monastic and lay contemplatives is *lectio divina* to provide an alternative culture to the world. We see that this third dimension, the dynamic ascetical life, takes a lifetime. This is done consciously and ceaselessly. There is never a time when we are awake that we are not attending to our practices. This third dimension with the moral voice is our personal willingness to relate to God. It moves our personal desires into an actual, loving relationship with God. This is prayer. To expect prayer to be abiding and effective without a moral life is disconnected with being a human person. We have many pulls away from a moral life because of our human condition, yet God's grace is sufficient. So, to work backward, first, I confessed my sins and put behind me personal sin. Then we seek an environment conducive to the moral life to stay in a wholesome relationship with ourselves, others, and God.

The Human Condition

I now return to my *lectio* with the book of Jonah. Was I hesitant in repenting and changing my life because of limitations I inherited from family? Was Jonah simply depressed? Did he have a bipolar condition or some other mitigating chemistry that prevented him from trusting and heeding God's word?

Maybe Jonah had a genetic condition or was mentally ill-suited to be the prophet to the Ninevites. Was he too prejudiced against his social enemies to invite them to conversion? The actual text about Jonah reports no conversion on his part. He got depressed when the repentance caused God's oracle of doom to be canceled. The Ninevites were saved, and they were Gentiles.

I have done a lot of inner work through the doors of psychology. Limitations from heredity, environment, and personal habits condition my responses in both taking action and also living with the consequences.

I also did some assessment of limitations because of my previous conditioning. I do not expect any level of a prayer or ascetical life to change my genetic code, but I did my homework on how to change my brain—how it thinks, the content of its thinking. I started taking seriously the fact that I can change my mind through practice (and God's grace). The practices that back out my selfishness and cultivate selflessness actually root out a propensity toward anger, depression, and vainglory.[6]

At first I was willing to say that I grew out of immature patterns, but now I am not so sure that I could have just as well grown more ruthlessly angry or pervasively depressed. I am proposing that this third dimension of *lectio divina* is just this kind of work: to retrain our brains, to back out our former way of thinking that is purely mental and replace those habits with ceaseless prayer and practices of faith as imaged in our gospels.

It seems to me that there are not two programs of self-improvement—one developmental through stages of human development and the other our religious training of asceticism. Are they not one and the same? Our early monastic tradition guides us and certainly does not negate the good we find in this therapeutic culture of caring and engaged compassion.

There is, however, one huge difference to report. The spiritual life under the river is a current that moves us, quickens us with the Holy Spirit. It may or may not assist us with health, wholeness, or wellness. It seems that the life cycle is birth and death, not a steady state of happiness. Joy, yes, but happiness, fitness, and wholeness, no. There are always some traces of an achy heart on this side of God's reign. We are not there—yet. Getting ahead of the story for a moment, though, I can report that afflictions can be extirpated, that is, rooted out. We can be free from the drag, the force of gravity that seemed to be habitual. We can change and no longer have that abiding hook toward anger, depression, grasping for things, etc. We can be at peace as an abiding way of being in this world here and now. *Lectio divina* is a way of getting into and of this peace. *Lectio divina* is the way to take that spiritual journey.

So back to Jonah: Is it my environment that prevents me from hearing and heeding the word of the Lord? Or is it my American culture that so limits my options? Can I do what Antony did when he heard the gospel mandate to follow his call from God? Antony, said to be the father of monasticism, heard the gospel mandate about selling all and following Jesus. He sold his farm and fled to the nearby desert.[7]

Can I be free enough to simply disengage from my family or origins, my outreach, my many friends and associates, my projects and contracted engagements? Perhaps the word of the Lord should come around in my next realm on the way to what we call heaven! Our belief in purgatory admits that there are other realms before our destination in heaven.

Again, as contrived as this sounds, here I am deep in the belly of the great fish, and I feel from the inside the dilemma of Jonah, whomever he might have been to the Ninevites. How can I go God's way while implanted in my culture: growing up American in rural Indiana and now living as a nun in an urban monastery in Beech Grove?

Three Ascetical Forms

To answer this, I returned to the monastic way of life—the culture under the river of the monastery. What forms did I uncritically bring with me from my former way of life? What forms in the monastery did I observe but not practice? Or what practices did I routinely do but not with *praxis* (the inner engagement of my mind)?

Three forms became my *lectio* work for this third voice, the moral voice:

1. the cell
2. manual labor
3. the habit

The Cell

As humans, we need a place for our bodies to reside, our emotions to empty, our souls to thrive. We need a place to be alone where we are not at risk from unwanted in-breaking noise, demands of relationships, or multiple obligations. We need a place to practice, to cultivate our inner peace to be ready for another day of work and outreach. Today, when travel is so easy and there are electric lights around the clock, we lose touch with the rhythm of daily, weekly, seasonal, and yearly cycles. In order not to get dizzy, we need to fix our eyes like a ballet dancer or a whirling dervish. The cell fixes us to be in the same place, at the same time, in the same sequence of our routines. The name for this fixed abode for the sake of God is "a cell." The cell is where we do our inner practice because we can descend our mind into our heart and watch our thoughts, guard our heart, cultivate the Jesus Prayer, practice colloquy, etc.

For optimum benefit of a cell for spiritual practice these criteria are helpful:

1. uncluttered
2. all things necessary
3. not too much
4. not too little
5. beautiful
6. designed harmony
7. moderate comfort
8. personal care necessities
9. no visitors (personal cloister)

10. enough light
11. enough air flow
12. enough heating/cooling
13. a bed
14. a writing table
15. a chair for study/meditation
16. soft light for reading
17. candle
18. storage for books/clothes
19. icon
20. elemental
21. efficient, not busy
22. quiet
23. enclosed by cloister
24. close to church
25. closed door
26. safe
27. minimal
28. still, never messy
29. proximate to bathroom
30. soft space

Some of us work out of our assigned bedrooms because we have no office. I have a rolling library cart to put work things out of sight in my room so that I can have full benefit of my cell as a place, space, and time for practice. In many monasteries the cells are adequate but far from ideal. For us to improve the practice of the cell that we have been assigned to, it would be good to review the spiritual idea behind a cell. To have a cell is to leave home and leave the way of the world that tends to make the bedroom an entertainment center. A cell is an ascetical practice for the sake of training the mind, body, and soul for prayer. As austere as this sounds, a deep abiding joy is the fruit of the practice of the cell. Again, the elders remind us that this is a practice and it cannot be understood except by doing it.

A cell is a symbol of the three days and three nights in the belly of the whale where we come to our senses and return to God. We listen to God's voice, and, instead of a hardened heart, we listen with the ear of our heart. We hear the directive and turn our whole life in that direction: to heed the word of the Lord. Then, if called again, we speak the word of the Lord to whomever we are sent. This is our vocation. Given that we shift and regress so often, the cell provides us with that "whale time" on a daily basis:

1. To practice the cell is first of all to have one single place to be alone. Second, the practice is to be in the cell every night and the in-between times of one's day. It's a default place to be and be alone.

2. Being in the cell is not unlike being in one's choir stall: set. The settling is done through posture, breathing, and stilling the mind. The posture is standing before one's icon, bowing before the image of Christ or Mary, lying on one's bed before sleep and upon awakening. The breathing is

noticed as the work is done; the exertion has completed its cycle, and the relief is relaxing.

3. The "stilling of the mind" is to gather the senses, come to one's self, and notice the mind's eye and where it is focused.

4. To practice the cell is to have one place where it is all right to be alone. That's the plan, the preferred way of being close and in one's skin. The walls provide boundaries that comfort and zone the radius of privacy and personal recollection.

5. To practice the cell is to have one place where so many years of practice compel prayer to rise spontaneously, ceaselessly, and harmoniously. The lit candle flickers, darts before the icon with a familiar odor of burnt offering.

6. To practice the cell is to have a place where simplicity reigns. The few things fit, and the space is uncluttered.

7. To practice the cell is to have one place where memory is sweet. Failures round details, smooth out wrinkles, flatten shiny grains of sand: no matter weighs heavily in this sphere. Ultimate concerns thrive here.

8. To practice the cell is to have one place where prayer happens upon waking and still drifts along at dusk. The sleep is consciously taken toward another more promising lifetime.

9. To practice the cell is most of all just being here, after all day being there. Death dies daily when we know we already have the seeds of eternal life here among the living.

10. To practice the cell is all about God—God "with us" in this tabernacle. Or is it a tent that can be moved about? Is the cell God, so that I am in God when I am in my cell? Or is God my cell so that God is in me when I am in my cell?

11. To practice the cell is to sit inside, knowing that it will teach me everything. This makes sense if I have done hours and hours of study and meditation on a text. It is the place where I memorize the psalms and passages of Scripture I want to carry around in my heart. If I have done this in my cell, then when I return time and time again the walls will remind me of those hallowed words.

12. To practice the cell and notice the cycles of days, months, seasons, years, and lifetimes is holy.

Manual Labor

A second ascetical practice that retrains my brain is manual labor. The teaching on manual labor is easy to write but so, so difficult to do! Manual labor has for its purpose to train the mind to actively disengage from its preoccupation with the ego-self and shift all attention and strength toward another.

To make this shift in consciousness to the other, it is best if the labor is routine, repetitive, unseen, certainly not noticed, and not ever completed just to get it done.

The satisfaction of manual labor is in the doing. It is an existential experience of being without an object of praise or comfort.

The test of it is that praise and blame are equal emotional experiences; starts and stops are according to another's will rather than determined by the self. That kind of work has difficulties as well as moments of success. Both are to gather no attachment. This is the training in selfless service. Praise and blame are all the same. Glory is given to God. God's grace prevails to offset mistakes. Errors are attributed to oneself, and excellence is given to God. If this seems harsh, it need not be so: we return to the gratitude of being creatures before our Creator and realize that of ourselves we are nothing, but through God's grace we are gifted and even made holy.

The test of manual labor as a practice is to start and stop. To start over when necessary, without any inner commentary, purifies the mind. We learn detachment from our ego and self-made thoughts. To be shifted to another duty at the will of another is a test of our indifference to self-glory and willingness to offer sacrifice to the Lord.

Manual labor is not toil, as in suffering. Work is prayer, and prayer is work. Joy casts out dread and anxiety.

Yes, this is monastic obedience. To do the will of another and to take the lowest place is obedience in the Rule. The best manual labor has no title, status, or prerequisites, such as a personal workshop or studio.

Manual labor is living out of humility to contribute to the whole—as in working for one's daily bread—and to refrain from creating a zone of particularity that grows and nurtures the ego. All is done for the honor and glory of God. All is done physically and not just thought about as a goal, or aspiration. Manual labor has no capacity for virtual reality.

The earliest monastics were not sponsored by society but worked by using their hands. The freedom of the mind to be attentive to ceaseless prayer and the present moment of doing what one is doing is a liberation that frees one to be alone with the Alone. In community, the manual labor is in service of the community that gifts us to be toward God together.

There is a tipping point when a monastic is abused by a superior, an elder, or a coworker. Emotional and/or sexual abuse is harmful to one's equilibrium and causes anger, depression, confusion, and emotional stress that prevents right relationship and productive work. We know it is not good for another person's soul to harm another, and we need not be harmed.

Reading the desert elders almost two thousand years later we don't consider ourselves above our master, but we also know that some forms of harsh treatment are simply the pathology of the one put in charge. This needs to be examined in the light, and action on behalf of justice needs to be taken. Some harsh sayings in the desert tradition need to be ignored in our times if they lead to deliberate bullying or belittling. Respect for directors and managers needs to be mutual and well-ordered for works and participants. Justice and compassion prevail through dialogue and sincere efforts to meet both group and individual needs.Today we see no benefit of contrived testing of a novice to make it harder for her. Elders simply work side by side and bring to the task openness and sincere joy at being able and willing to work according to one's ability and capacity.

Outer practice should be ordinary work and inner *praxis* is the intention and single-mindedness to attend to God's presence and one's calling to do the work with wholesome generosity and cooperation. As hard as the practice of manual labor is, the *praxis* is even more difficult: the *praxis* (what you do with your mind while you are doing the practice) is to bring total attention to the doing of the task. No commentary. No thoughts about it, about the worker or the boss insisting on the work being done. This non-thought is the *praxis*: to shift into no thinking about anything whatsoever. There is a deeper level of being in action that is called for here.

When we go deep, there are two experiences that fast forward the realization of God's presence: one is meditation where all thinking is suspended, and we sit in the silence that is at work in us; the other is manual labor where we rest our thinking minds and do those repetitive actions that have for their product union with God.

Manual labor is not optional, but it certainly can be more than functional. We can work with our hands doing this inner *praxis* of the mind not only while we are working but also to train our brains to stay firm in the doing. Firm action that is on behalf of others rather than in service to the self is the kind of work contemplatives specialize in doing.

The training of the mind is an amazing discovery; it goes back to the ancient Greek philosophers. The mind can become steady, focused, and freely given. The drag of dissipation, emotional drama, and reluctant service can be eliminated and replaced with work—simply doing what I am doing. Deep, satisfying joy follows. Soon I have the personal experience of my work being my prayer and my prayer being my work.

In Buddhism another name for a monk is "to be content." That fits our mission of stilling our mind, body, and soul and being at rest in this world abiding with God. We are content. There is a time for strenuous striving, but there is also a time to be content and to rest and relax into the promises of God's presence, not only in the next life, but now.

Perhaps Jonah's mind was so conditioned that he saw all work as dread, doom, and gloom. He needed to rest in the hold of the ship, the belly of the whale, the depth of the sea. I do think that monastic practices of the cell and manual labor bring us up, up, up to the altar of adoration and joyful service.

Perhaps the lack of form is what keeps me from sustaining resolve. The canticle in chapter 2 of Jonah is contrite, respectful, and grateful. But soon, and very soon, he is his irritated self once again. We need forms to lock in and stabilize our resolve.

The Habit

Another such form is the monastic habit. American religious are divided about this ancient form of dress for women dedicated to consecrated life. Personally, I find that without the form of a habit I have difficulty keeping my portable cell with me. Because of the human condition, I tend to take on habits and customs of the environment or culture that surrounds me. Some form of a habit would be helpful, but certainly it does not have to be the full garb that I wore in my early years in the monastery. While the veil is a symbol in many cultures, I do not find it essential. But where is the dialogue to consider the habit?

I offer ten starting points to give voice to the sensitive question of what women should wear.

1. As Vatican II suggested, religious women need to return to the spirit of their founders. These communities were a vast array of stouthearted, gifted souls. The largest group of American women religious were founded to do apostolic works. These so-called modern congregations were missioned to do works in education, hospitals, social services, evangelization, and special services to immigrants. While in their formative years they took on the clothes of the women of their times to do their outreach to the poor, they were soon legislated by the church to keep those particular styles of dress as normative. The example of the Daughters of Charity founded by St. Vincent de Paul and Louise de Marillac had this directive in 1633:

   [The sisters shall have] for monastery only the houses of the sick and the place where the Superioress resides,

> for cell a hired room, for chapel the parish church, for
> cloister the streets of the city, . . . for grill the fear of
> God, for veil holy modesty.[8]

2. The earlier monastic tradition prescribed a habit. *Institute* 1 of John Cassian's writings is titled "The Garb of the Monks." It is eleven chapters of what to wear. He talks about the belt, garment, hoods, colobia (cloak), cords, fabric, staff, footwear, and adaptations for climate conditions. In *Institute* 4.5 Cassian states:

> Hence, when someone has been received, all his former
> possessions are removed from him, such that he is not
> even permitted to have the clothing that he wore. He
> is brought to the council of the brothers, stripped of
> what is his in their midst, and clothed in the garb of the
> monastery at the hands of the abba. . . . Thenceforth,
> knowing that he will be clothed and fed from there,
> he will learn both to possess nothing and never to be
> worried about the morrow, according to the words of
> the Gospel, and he will not be ashamed to be on a par
> with the poor—that is, with the body of the brother-
> hood—among whom Christ was not ashamed to be
> numbered and whose brother he did not blush to call
> himself; rather he will glory in having become the com-
> panion of his servants.

The habit is a symbol of no rank and that the wearer is in solidarity with the poor.

3. The Rule of Benedict prescribes a habit after a full year of formation as a novice. Then, during the

profession rite the old clothes are stripped and turned in. In chapter 55 of the Rule of Benedict is a description of the habit and few possessions: "that is, cowl, tunic, sandals, shoes, belt, knife, stylus, needle, handkerchief and writing tablets" (55.19). These things are bestowed by the monastery and received by the monk.

4. The habit is more than a disciplinary regulation that keeps order and maintains a balance of needs and wants. From the earliest times, the clothing was symbolic of inner desires and outward resolve.

5. The habit is given from an elder. We know that Benedict was clothed with a monastic habit by the monk Romanus.[9] Evagrius was received and clothed by Malenia. There's a sacred lineage that has its history from one generation to the next through the investiture rituals. So it's not so much what is handed on as the garments, though it should possess symbolic value. What seems significant is to receive the confirmation of the vows from someone who has lived the life and kept the vows in an earlier generation. The habit is the symbol of having kept the vows and the intent of keeping them so to hand them over to another generation.[10]

6. History testifies that there are two distinct religious charisms in the church. One is the monastic way of life, and the other is the apostolic religious life. Both take lifetime vows and both are vocations, but the older tradition of monasticism is different from

the apostolic way of life. From the early Christian era until about 1600 all women religious were considered to be monastic. Monastic charism enjoys a habit, cloister, obedience under a superior, prayer, and work with no required outside employment or ministry. The church officials restricted travel of women, their governance over properties, their dress, their customs, and their sacramental access. The rise of the apostolic communities who were founded to assist the poor and reach out to the marginal left the cloister to do so. These communities of women took on the dress of the local people and were known by their good works.

7. The monastic nuns continued living in monasteries, mostly in Europe. In the early and mid-1800s many Benedictine nuns were recruited to America to serve the ethnic populations that emigrated from their home country. For example, Benedictine sisters came to Ferdinand, Indiana, to serve the needs of the German immigrants in southern Indiana. The many well-written stories of the foundations from Europe to America document the dual struggle of monastic observances and sponsoring apostolic institutions. Both require presence and regular work hours. In his Rule, Benedict envisioned a self-contained monastery where most members would live and work. Traveling and working away from the monastery was the exception, not the rule. The monastic schedule takes precedence in

the monastery, and apostolic outreach conforms to this schedule. The apostolic way of life views such observance differently. Apostolic communities fit the schedule of work and prayer around the needs of the people who require services. The apostolic religious resided and worked for the sake of the mission. The monastic way of life is the mission for Benedictines and Cistercians.

In America, when Vatican II suggested sisters return to the spirit of the founder, there was an overwhelming impetus for Benedictine sisters to restart from the genetic moment of coming to the United States as a worker with an apostolic mission rather than return to the original intent in the Rule of Benedict. The original charism of Benedict came with the first sisters who arrived and is here today. For us to return to the spirit of our founder not only means doing social services but also transplanting a monastic life of seeking God through a distinctive contemplative life that inculturates the desert tradition in America.

This difference between monastic and apostolic orders in the church has been parsed out over and over with discussions of the distinction between nuns and sisters, solemn and simple vows, active and contemplative life. For the purpose of retrieving the observance of a habit, I am making the point that the more apostolic work one does, the more it makes sense to wear lay clothes and be lay workers side by side with all others. The more monastic one is, the more sense it makes to wear a distinctive garb that symbolizes the lineage and identity of the community—a portable cell for the fierce inner work of asceticism and community rigors. It seems that a distinction is needed to retrieve, reclaim, and reappropriate for American Benedictine monastic women so we can discern some form of a habit that expresses and constitutes the monastic way of life but doesn't reclaim the hubris of the religious garb from the Middle Ages.

8. Dress for women is a deeply psychological expression of gender, taste, sensitivity, and individual artistic expression of texture, color, style, and grace of presentation. What women wear is not a casual decision. Women make a conscious choice.[11] Clothes are functional to a point but mostly an external vehicle of identity. The clothes women wear are put on selectively. There's an expression of oneself with clothes and also an initiative of conversation with others. Monastic dress can say, "I am here for you," or, "I understand your culture."

9. After Vatican II there was also a new autonomy for women religious. Starting with the Sister Formation Conference in 1954 and the emergence of the Leadership Conference of Women Religious in the 1970s, there were many gatherings of religious women. Identity as an entity distinct from male clerics and religious solidified as self-determining

and organized groups of women. Men could no longer mandate what clothes were worn or how and when women should wear them.

10. Yet, what still needs to be established for monastic women is a practice of a habit that is given by a wise elder, as in a lineage like priesthood. Monastic women would do well to have a simple dress that expresses vows of stability, obedience, and conversion to the monastic way of life as well as presents a woman's concern and work on behalf of the poor and marginalized. The nun needs a portable cell that can preserve vows as well as express zeal. Our identity in the monastic tradition is more than a consecration to dedicate our lives to serve the marginalized and poor. Monastics have an ontic identity of irreversible vow to pray always and to live the monastic way of life under an abbot and a rule. It is an alternative vocation to lay living through the domestic arrangements we call home. The monastic way of life has form and forces that are explicitly religious in symbol and fact.

So what defines monastic life? Is it a combination of the above? Is it just a common experience of a common seeking or a common goal? Do we need the form of a habit? Would the habit, along with the cell and manual labor, hold us to our vow to pray without ceasing?

In summary, we have three ascetical practices in service of our *lectio divina*: We remain in our cell. We do manual labor. We carry our cell with us when we wear the monastic habit. Monastics have forms in service of the contemplative life. But what are the forms for lay-persons living with family and in work situations? At our School of *Lectio Divina* in Beech Grove we gave teachings on many of our monastic forms: cell, refectory, cloister, etc. Then we asked the lay participants to give some consideration to their contemplative forms in their homes, workplaces, and in-between times. The creativity was astonishing: each person found in ordinary life ways and means to observe solitude, practice silence, and train the mind through *praxis*. It's my hope in this book that the monastic forms can give support to the lay seeker to find domestic forms that would help him or her to do *lectio divina* in this sustained method.

Chapter 5

More on How We Get There from Here: Further Teaching on the Moral Dimension

The third dimension of *lectio*, which is the moral voice heard by the personal senses, is hard work. I do not want to be like Jonah. I want to change, repent, and pay my vows to the Lord. I can now close the book, my Bible. I've got the message. This inner work is my responsibility. I no longer can simply meditate out there about somebody else. I am everyone in the story. I again invoke the Holy Spirit to help me shift from thinking to watching my thoughts to praying. The revelatory text now has done its thing, and I must do my work. This is the heart of *Lectio Divina*: to face God's directives. This is my encounter with the living God.

Again, the best way for me to teach it in this book is simply to continue to provide an outline of how to

proceed. After confession and cultivating ceaseless repentance I had that raw experience that my need for
God's mercy was acute but also I needed help to prevent
those conditions that caused me to be like Jonah. The
practices of the cell and manual labor are ongoing and
provide a stable place for me to practice. The watching of
my thoughts, guard of the heart, and staying awake (as
in vigils) are demanding. I certainly found the benefit
of monastic forms, such as the habit,[1] that hold me in a
culture of selflessness rather than my former way of life
that was "selfing" in all manner of projects and relationships. I need a culture that is an alternative to the world.
But even in the monastic culture I need much more help.

While I had renounced my former way of life, I did
not have a sturdy monastic way of life to replace it. I
renounced thoughts of my former way of life as in the
second renunciation but replicated a similar set of afflictions in the monastic life, just as I had done in my
former life. For the sake of this book on *lectio divina*, I
will take up two afflictions that were obstacles for me:
anger and vainglory.

Reducing the Afflictions

Why do one's afflictions need to be confronted for the
sake of the spiritual life? What can we do? We can look
to the practices that reduce the affliction and the *praxis*
(what you do with your mind while you are practicing
restraint) that prevents the affliction from rising again.

The human condition prevents us from easy conversions, but it does provide the sturdy ways of living a virtuous life. This is another way of saying it is quite beneficial for us to use our suffering as our skillful means toward purity of heart. This is all part of sustained *lectio*. We now consider two real afflictions, anger and vainglory. Then, we will provide a teaching on discernment:

1. Anger can be reduced and rooted out by manifesting thoughts. Anger can be prevented by ceaseless prayer practice like the Jesus Prayer.
2. Vainglory can be reduced and rooted out by the practice of recollection and prevented by the practice of colloquy or other practices like the Little Way of Saint Thérèse.

The way of life that integrates the spiritual life with the outer human journey is the practice of discernment. Without discernment we risk that our practices can do more harm than good. This is why we need to receive spiritual direction from wise elders or to stay close to the teachings of our tradition. Discernment is learned as a skillful means to hear and heed the word of God. We can consider these two examples, one about undergoing treatment for cancer and the other about requesting to become a hermit. These examples of typical decisions show the connection with confessing our sins, manifesting our thoughts, and being in spiritual direction with a wise elder.

We see that the moral voice not only provides directives given to Jonah but also gives me mandates through ordinary invitations to hear the word of the Lord and heed his voice.

Anger Prevents Prayer

A recurring affliction I have suffered through is anger. It matters not the cause; it comes and I am confronted with anger's insidious ability to infect my mind. I will insert here a teaching from John Cassian[2] on anger. Surprisingly, this teaching is found not in *Institute* 8, "On Anger," but in *Conference* 16, "On Friendship." There are many teachings in this one conference. A dominant theme is the way anger is harmful to relationships with others and God.

Teaching from Cassian

I read *Conference* 16 in great depth and for every detail, noting the many teachings. The strongest admonitions are these three:

1. Others are required for our virtuous life so we are just not in our heads thinking to ourselves and fully intoxicated with self. Recall St. Basil's, "Whose feet would you wash?"
2. The biggest obstacle to enduring friendships that are images of God's love and compassion is to be angry or not to forgive those who are angry toward

me. I need to learn loving ways to replace hostility with dialogue. Replace judgment with compassion.

3. The science of friendship is to will and refuse the same thing. The most important object of friendship is far beyond treasuring each other; rather, it is to have the opportunity of support on the journey toward renunciation and to live nothing less than toward God. So both have to be on the journey inside. This journey is one of renunciation.

The sections on anger are explicit: I see that I must never be angered for any reason, whether just or unjust. I can calm the anger that my friend may have against me, even if it is groundless. Reflect daily on the fact that I am going to depart from this world. Holding all things in common removes potential differences. Remove causes for anger.[3] Then, I can act from the heart with compassion.

This is the third dimension of *lectio divina*: to personally do what the text says to do. It is imperative. In wisdom literature as a genre, there is no grasping of the content unless it is experienced in my life. Soon I get the teaching but need something more to implement it. A teaching just doesn't get me there. I can know it. I can will it, but unless I retrain my mind[4] to back out the thoughts that move up the chain of anger I will fail to heed by doing the word. Anger is an obstacle to relationships, especially in community life. Boundaries that prevent anger are helpful to preserve harmony.[5]

Recommended Practice to Reduce Anger: Manifestation of Thoughts to a Wise Elder[6]

To disclose our hearts to a wise elder is to dash our thoughts on the rock that is Christ (RB 7.44; 4.50). The Greek term is *exagoreusis*. For us, it is simply to lay out the risings of the thoughts rather than tell the story or get involved in the content. Here is a sample of what it might look like. The topic is anger. Both the elder and the one confessing thoughts need to know what the method is. There are two roles. The elder listens attentively; asks no clarifying questions; refrains from engaging in conversation, making comments, or trying to console the person disclosing her thoughts. The one disclosing comes prepared for the session and might even have a written list of thoughts. She refrains from deviating from the list of thoughts that are rising and needing to be manifested to a wise elder. The person disclosing her thoughts images the thoughts as toxic entities that need to leave the body and the mind, so this sharing is simply to list in any order what comes to mind.

So here is the list of thoughts manifested in about ten minutes of uninterrupted presence of the elder.

> *Example: Anger*
> I feel restless.
> In choir I can't keep my mind on the moment.
> I continue to judge the pace, pitch, and balance of
>   the choir.

I find a couple of voices most irritating.
I cope by zoning out.
Sometimes I don't sing.
My silence though is more like pouting.
I am also irritated when people make noises.
Some have chronic coughs.
Some who read have poor diction and phrasing.
I am mostly angry at "X."
That voice is most dominating.
Is there nothing that can be done?
I find that I'm so angry with that person.
I don't sit at table or converse with that person.
I find all manner of distaste.
I have had this situation for several years now.
It is not getting any better.

Then, in silence, the whole list is received. No need to discuss the content. The point is to clear the mind and to let rise the impulse of the Holy Spirit who will console, coach, and warm from underneath. The Spirit will give courage and fortitude to get through the tough time. The elder prays in her heart during the disclosure. Notice there is no admonition against anger. This very disclosure is doing something about the anger in the spirit of repentance. There is also no absolving of the anger. The process is to move the anger out of one's consciousness so that the light of the Holy Spirit can rise and direct the person to the next invitation to grace. When we are angry, we are blind. Repentance returns our sight.

If a word comes to the elder, she shares it; if not, the two simply end with a shared prayer, maybe the Our Father, and part with a blessing from the elder.

This disclosure is relatively brief. It's best if there are short times each day or each week to manifest. If the two know each other well, it could just be an e-mail or a short phone conversation. The point is to raise up the thought and dash it out and refrain from any reinforcement of the affliction of anger. Discernment will provide the right action when the fire of anger cools.

If there is some necessary conversation to have with the elder, that shift into a discussion should be clearly a separate part of the session so as not to lose the effectiveness of disclosing the anger. In the light we see light.[7] In our minds we tend to circle round and round and go up the chain of agitation and indignation. Instead, we lay out our thoughts promptly. If we do not accompany them with further thoughts, they mellow and whimper away. One manifests thoughts with a disposition of repentance or with the abiding disposition of *penthos* (longing for God's mercy).

There are three major differences, however, between manifesting thoughts and confessing sins. First, the nature of sin is a violation of conscience. I confess that I did wrong. Manifesting thoughts is simply the naming of thoughts one after the other. They are rising thoughts, and if identified early, often, and willingly these thoughts have very little power over my will. I am not my thoughts.

A second difference is that, when we are manifesting thoughts, it is not recommended that we return to the past. This practice is a tool to see my thoughts "now" and to lay them out so that they have no more power over me. St. Benedict says that we are to dash them on the rock that is Christ. Confession is naming a past thought, word, or deed that was done and is now regretted.

A third difference is that confession is a sacrament administered by an ordained priest. It has a history, a ritual, and a symbolic meaning that is shared by Catholic Christians. The sacrament is experienced in the context of the larger ecclesial community. Disclosure of thoughts can be done with mutual friends on the spiritual journey, or a superior, or a spiritual director.

Manifestation of thoughts is for the ongoing work of a contemplative. It's a monastic practice that is regularly done to get at the earliest level of thought and not the end-stage result of sin. The devotional confession seeks the grace of the sacrament—forgiveness of sin—whereas manifestation of thoughts does not.

This tradition of disclosure to a wise elder got replaced with the confession of sin that was the end stage of the thoughts that became emotions and passions. The emphasis on confession of sin was one factor, but the other historical fact that contributed to the loss of this tradition was that the appointment of abbots and prioresses was done more and more by the reigning aristocracy and for the purpose of administration of the monastery. Managers replaced elders.

The position of elder in some Eastern traditions was passed down in the nonelected role of a *staretz*, but in the West the practice of manifestation of thoughts was simply supplanted and/or forgotten.

Can we have confidence in this old tradition from the Christian East, *exagoreusis*? Perhaps it is happening more than we know. St. Benedict recommended this tool (RB 7.44; 4.50). It follows from the teachings on the eight thoughts that there are tools to reduce these afflictions. If there is a wise elder in our midst, we lay out our thoughts simply and humbly. We also ask her for tools that could help us.

As we know, we are not our thoughts, but they can trick us into compulsive habits. So we need to lay them out in the light. Watch them in the presence of a wise elder who can also watch us watching our thoughts. In our solitude, we do this practice of guarding our hearts, but it is good to root out afflictions with the humility practice of disclosure in the light, in the presence of another's light that is not obscured. Their very own light (presence) can heal. Again, this is the earliest form of the sacrament of reconciliation.

Anatomy of a Thought

Let's review the anatomy of a thought and how it starts and gains strength and sways us into action. This list is helpful because if we can catch our thoughts early, often, and as gently as we can we will be able to refrain from the energies of the afflictions that cloud our discrimination. This is the first stage of discernment: sorting our thoughts, watching them rise, noticing that we are not our thoughts. Let's review the sequence again:

1. The thought rises.
2. An image appears.
3. The dialogue of my mind is accompanied by an image.
4. This evolves into and invitation (a) to continue the dialogue or (b) to refrain from the same.
5. I consent to the inner promptings of further imaging and conversation inside my head accompanied by feelings.
6. The thought gets solid and offers a suggestion to take action.
7. I either take action or refrain from the invitation/temptation.
8. There's a simultaneous melody line that is another conversation with the thought and the person in this thinking mode about intention/motivation; tradition calls this the "second thought."
9. I act on the invitation one time.
10. I continue in that direction of the original prompting (an affliction).
11. I continue being engaged with that thought that is now an entity accompanied by emotion (passion).
12. I act often in collaboration with the passionate emotion and it becomes a habit (pattern).

13. I then dwell in that ethos of suffering (*pathos*) until
14. this entity becomes my identity (captivity).
15. I am the thought!

A Second Approach of the Process of Manifestation of Thoughts (Disclosure) to a Wise Elder

1. Lay out thought without commentary to be heard in the light.
2. Back out the affliction as early as possible.
3. The usual ones are food, sex, things, anger, dejection, *acedia*, vainglory, and pride.
4. Aim to keep vigilant so as to be prepared for the entities to rise.
5. Aim to manifest the affliction as often as it rises.
6. Be not surprised if the affliction rises with more emotion earlier and faster, with subtle promptings.
7. Refrain from inner dialogue with the affliction rising, especially self-justification and rationalizations.
8. Refrain from daydream-like fantasy of either memories or plans to do such an encounter in the future.
9. Confess with compunction of heart.

This tradition is all but lost but can be retrieved by any and all of us. Like all practices, the only way to learn it is by doing it. It seems to me that what is most helpful is to start with someone to manifest to, and if that person isn't the right one, then God sees the sincere heart and the right one will appear.

The key is to resist analysis, commentary, and contextual drama. The point is to observe the thoughts early to catch the origin of the rising thought. We see that the process is the content rather than just a method to get at the drama. For example, the monk ought to be not angry but calm and live in an abiding peace. It isn't really helpful to review the story line of the anger over and over again. It only serves to retraumatize the seeker into deeper and deeper grooves of the affliction. This process is to observe how the thought of anger seduces me in the negative cycle of harm, harmed, and harmer (violence, victim, victimizer). The only attention we need to pay to trauma is to make sense of it, that is, to make peace and not resist it. We remember that it happened, not all the commentary. The goal is repentance and *conversatio* of our way of life.

In conclusion, it seems to me that in our times we cannot afford to lose touch with this tradition of disclosure of our thoughts to a wise elder. It will open the door of our salvation and peace of heart.[8]

The process of manifestation of thoughts goes like this: each day the person writes down the recurring thoughts that rise over and over again. This list is the beginning of the old practice of examination of conscience. Again, if one can write down the earliest form of the rising of the thought, the better the practice serves one to grasp the cycle and redirect the energies.

Then, periodically, the person shares these thoughts with a wise elder who receives them—simply receives them and watches the thoughts from her view without judgment or scolding. If an inspired word rises from within the elder, then a word is shared; if not, the manifestation of consciousness is received, and the elder simply gives the practitioner a blessing. The process is routine, and sometimes the practitioner has the same list over and over again.

Eventually, the affliction subsides when it's not fed with worry, aggravation, condemnation, or commentary. It seems that the only kind of thoughts that the elders discouraged the practitioner from sharing were memories of sins that had already been forgiven. To give them room is to risk depression and despair of God's mercy.

I wrote this poem that reads the canticle of Jonah as a triumph over interior afflictions. The hidden meaning of the story is my moral life. Running away from my conversion. This verse is a meditation, yes, but it came to me after many years of interior asceticism. Here, in the moral dimension of *lectio divina* the burning bush emerges as my encounter with God.

> *Being Bowed Over*
> I called to the Lord in my distress
> over and over again . . .
> Rescued, over and over again . . .
> Was headed where I thought was the Lord's
>   directive
> and returned on dry land to walk
> over and over again as if the first time
> free of drag and driven-ness.

> Is the lesson to prevent trauma
> or to learn from it
> and to stand in
> a permanent bow of respect?

What backs out anger is manifestation of thoughts, but what keeps anger from returning to our consciousness is ceaseless prayer. In the Christian tradition there is the most powerful prayer that uproots our anger and plants seeds of our desire for God: the Jesus Prayer. So to prevent anger we saturate our consciousness with the name of Jesus. We can enter the trap that the Jesus Prayer keeps anger at bay, but then we'll start thinking about God. Thinking, even about God, must be renounced as thoughts about God are simply thoughts. Our desire is to experience God, not our thoughts about God. But the starting place for this experience of God is ceaseless prayer.

Praxis of the Jesus Prayer/Prayer of the Heart[9]

Forms of the Jesus Prayer

The Jesus Prayer is a most important prayer practice for Christians who want to have an abiding consciousness of Christ. We should first pray to the Holy Spirit to teach us how to pray and also ask if this is the way of prayer for me. There are many doors into prayer, but this one has an ancient tradition that is reliable and available to us today. First, we need to see the words of the Jesus Prayer.

The Jesus Prayer has many forms:

- Jesus, Son of God, have mercy on me, a sinner.
- Jesus, Son of the Living God, have mercy on me, a sinner.
- Jesus, have mercy on me.
- Jesus, mercy.
- *Kyrie Eleison*.
- Jesus.

Teaching

When it is practiced over time and is a habit, on its own the prayer drops to the heart and becomes the habitual prayer of the heart. The teachings are rich: the invocation of the Holy Name of Jesus, which continues our baptismal immersion, brings our attention to Christ and Christ, in turn, dwells in us. The prayer warms the heart and becomes an experience of Presence. In the Christian East a *staretz* would caution the pilgrim that it takes assiduous practice.[10]

The practice of the Jesus Prayer will thrive unless we are living a life of sin. When we stray, we return immediately without hesitation. Resume the practice and it will be an aid to resist temptation in the future. The request for mercy is real. *Penthos* is an abiding state of remaining "in the need of God's mercy." With spiritual practices comes a clear, focused mind that can leap to vainglory without the sense of being "in need of God." Radically, to the core one feels the need of help! This is a sense of *penthos* or feeling compunction because of being a sinner.

Sometimes *penthos* is manifested by the gift of tears. These are wholesome tears, not morbid tears of depression.

After the Jesus Prayer becomes a habit, we can feel the full weight of how sad it is for Christians to use the name of the Lord in vain, to curse or swear lightly. The Presence is a felt blessing. Who are we to judge, condemn, and call down wrath on another since we are no better?

For a fuller explanation and teachings about this tradition of the Jesus Prayer preserved in the Christian East, we have especially the writings of the *Philokalia*.[11] The dominant fruit of this practice of the Jesus Prayer that becomes prayer of the heart is that moment/place/space of contemplation experienced by each of us. A profound silence brings together our fragmented mind, and we become stable and attentive. After years of practice one can descend the mind into the heart "at will" and find that place of stillness. *Hesychia* is the technical term for the whole movement of contemplatives seeking the deep levels of solitude, silence, and stillness that is physical, emotional, and spiritual.[12]

A caution about the Jesus Prayer is that it is so powerful that it needs to be practiced by one under spiritual direction of some elder who also does the Jesus Prayer. Also, the Jesus Prayer is in the heart, but the whole person needs an entire set of worship and shared faith in community. To isolate the Jesus Prayer from the full practicing of the Christian life in the church is to miss the fullness of Jesus' teachings.

Let's return to the inner work of this third dimension of *lectio divina*. We've seen teachings, practices, and the need to be somewhat accountable to a wise elder if we are to avoid self-deception and sustain our practice. We see that the affliction of anger has many teachings that are compelling, but directives seem to fade quickly and we return to ordinary consciousness. This return can even lead to hardness of heart—even after the heart is stirred by many intimate graces from Our Lord. This anger can be backed out through the practice of manifestation of thoughts. Then, where the anger resided, the Jesus Prayer can restore the consciousness of God's presence.

So note the sequence here: (a) an affliction prevents prayer; (b) a teaching helps us to know that anger needs to be reduced, restrained, rooted out; but (c) we need a practice like the Jesus Prayer to prevent anger from rising in the first place.[13] We want a God consciousness rather than any other object, especially if that object in our consciousness is accompanied by the emotion of anger that goes up the chain of annoyance, irritation, agitation, retaliation, revenge, and rage. It can even become harm to self, as in suicide, or to another, as in murder.

For the sake of clarity, here is another example using the same sequence but with another affliction: I have experienced the recurrence of vainglory from time to time. First, I will provide a teaching on vainglory from the life of St. Teresa of Avila and then her recommended practice of recollection; finally, I would recommend the *praxis* of colloquy to maintain that consciousness of the humanity of Jesus. This consciousness orders all other relationships.

Obviously, there are other afflictions, practices, and teachings about the inner life of prayer, but these two offer a start. There is help in our Christian tradition to get out from underneath afflictions and return to an abiding childlike consciousness of God.

Affliction of Vainglory

I'm not sure if I have strayed from the book of Jonah or if while I am in the belly of the whale I have discovered the life and teachings of St. Teresa. She had an acute affliction of vainglory. She defined herself through the perception of what she thought others thought of her. She was vain rather than giving all honor and glory to God.

I continue this *lectio* with a comparison of my own lifelong experience of my self-centeredness versus a devotion to Jesus. I was born on the feast of the great St. Teresa. While I identified with her affliction, I also identified with her remedy. She learned to have total confidence in practicing recollection that obtained for her consciousness and mindfulness of Jesus ever-present as the risen Lord rather than relying on all her friends and benefactors.[14] As baptized Christians, we can expect liberation from both our sinfulness and our felt afflictions that burden us in our earthly life. The gospels are full of stories about how Jesus heals and comforts. Note the possessed man of the Gerasene territory (Mark 5:1-14).

We can learn from St. Teresa how she was confronted and healed by our Lord of her affective disorder.

Teaching from St. Teresa of Avila

Life of St. Teresa

She entered the convent, but the first eighteen years out of twenty-eight as a professed nun she was interiorly divided. She suffered the ambiguity of placing her heart in friendship with God *and* friendship with the world. She also suffered from disordered attachments: too much, too extreme, too fond, not only giving time and attention to the world's things, but also devoting her inner consciousness to others outside of herself. Her thoughts were consumed with engagement with the world "out there" and not with a serious practice of devotion to Christ in her heart. She was addicted and had many mutual dependencies.

Father Daniel Chowning, OCD, provides the following list of St. Teresa's issues:[15]

1. Teresa squandered time visiting, reading novels, building and sustaining friendships, and being carried along by culturally acceptable customs. She acted without discretion.
2. She was virtually and actually "in the world"; she lived outside of herself.
3. There was no intention to offend God, but she simply lived outside the sphere of memory of God.

4. The "world" was to live totally laterally on earth. The world she speaks of, which she considers to stand in opposition to God, is not so much earthly reality but rather her inner "world of affective reactions and contacts" that held her dependent and made her live outside herself.

5. But she also thirsted for God. Her great conflict: Teresa was unable to reconcile her need for human love and companionship with her thirst for God. She became divided and fragmented within herself, and a duality was set up between her longing for God and her need to give of herself in human relationship. Up until the age of thirty-nine, in the year 1554, this battle between the world and the spirit raged. In the early years she enjoyed being a nun. Then, for three years she was bedridden with an undiagnosed illness. She had become a nun, which was thought to be the path of virtue, but being a nun did not take her out of the world. So Teresa had the same conflict she had as a youth, divided from the world and God. There were no boundaries on her affect. The monastery did not help her.

Description of her monastery: It was a place where "worldly honors and recreations [were] so exalted and one's obligations so poorly understood . . . that [they took] for virtue what is sin" (*Life* 7.4)[16] When she asked her confessor, she received bad advice. They approved of her conduct and assured her that these "occasions and associations" would in no way harm her. She was in a state of captivity where there was no escape; when with God, she felt attachments to the world. She trusted in herself to overcome troubles instead of counting on God's mercy. She said she was searching for someone who could lead her to reconciliation and give peace to her restless, torn heart: "I wanted to live but I had no one to give me life, and I was unable to catch hold of it."

So, symptoms of this affliction or affective disorder would be these:

1. living vicariously through others
2. preoccupied with thinking about what others think of oneself
3. living a distracted, divided life
4. ongoing conversations with others rather than with Our Lord
5. going from pastime to pastime
6. ashamed to draw near to God
7. compartmentalizing

St. Teresa's Conversions

How did Teresa get out of her vainglory and into her mystical relationship with Christ? She discovered the prayer of recollection: the God she sought was not abstract or diffused but truly personal—the incarnate Word living within her. "I tried as hard as I could to keep Jesus

Christ, our God and our Lord, present within me, and that was my way of prayer" (*Life* 4.7). Through her love for Jesus, her love of neighbor also increased and she ordinarily avoided all faultfinding and speaking evil of anyone. She admitted her powerlessness one day during Lent 1554—her "much wounded Christ" compunction event (*Life* 9.1). She surrendered herself before the power of the risen Jesus. She opened herself to the saving and healing power of Jesus. The Lord himself freed her from herself, her habits. "It was in 1556 that He gave me freedom [*libertad*], that I, with all the efforts of many years, could not attain" (see *Life* 24.8).

She started to meditate on the humanity of Jesus Christ. "I started again to love the most sacred humanity" (*Life* 24.2). Her definitive conversion was after praying for some days the *Veni Creator*. After this definitive conversion she says of herself, "For I have never again been able to tie myself to any friendship or to find consolation or bear particular love for any other persons than those I understand love Him and strive to serve Him; nor is it in my power to do so, nor does it matter whether they are friends or relatives" (*Life* 24.5–7).

We see in her life that Jesus satisfied Teresa's hunger for love. He freed her from the crippling power and attraction others had exercised over her. In Jesus, Teresa found true satisfaction of heart. Through him, in him, she could love others without a sense of being split within herself or with scruples and interior struggles. Relationships would no longer necessarily appear in opposition to her search for God but would become important elements of the spiritual life. The difference was that Jesus Christ was the source of her warm and caring friendships. Teresa's conversion shifted her to a Jesus-centered awareness and awareness of Jesus as a friend. She is explicit that to love God was too vague, but to literally have Jesus of Nazareth is the Way. Teresa's discovery of the humanity of Jesus Christ thus gave her search for God a concrete form, and this, in turn, healed the division she experienced between her spirit that longed for God and her humanity that craved the earth. She no longer experienced her search for God in opposition to daily life or her humanity. Rather, it would be integrated into concrete bodily existence, for in Jesus, God has entered fully into human life and has become one of us.

During her time, the sixteenth century, spirituality taught that Jesus was a door to the Father, a stage along the way. It was taught that Jesus was an obstacle to perfect *contemplatio*. The spiritual person must leave aside all corporeal ideas and notions, even concerning the historical Christ, and remain absorbed in the divinity. Few, however, understood the humanity of Jesus as the abiding place where one dwells all along life's journey to God. If we are to arrive at the fullness of Christian maturity, we do so only in and through Jesus. If we are to knowingly and lovingly surrender to the mystery of God, this takes place in and through an abiding personal relationship with the Man-Jesus "in whom and in whom alone the immediacy of God is reached."[17] Teresa experienced the risen Christ, not in an esoteric way, but amid the realities of daily life. When she had to burn her treasured books: "I shall give you a living book" (*Life* 26.5). It was in 1572 (at the age of fifty-seven) during Eucharist when she experienced spiritual marriage. This, she says, has the purpose to free us to carry on Jesus' salvific mission of compassion. Through his sufferings our sufferings fortify us against our weakness so we can imitate him. We can see that for most of us this takes a lifetime. Teresa was born in 1515 and entered the monastery at the age of twenty-one; then, in 1545—a full nine years later— she had an encounter with the risen Lord, but it was another eleven years afterward, in 1556, that she converted her whole heart to the God of her vows, so that at the age of forty-one she became a true novice.

Because of her years of unfocused zeal and bad advice from her confessors she takes on those spiritual writers of her time who advised serious Christians in pursuit of holiness to set aside all corporeal notions, representations, ideas, and thoughts in prayer, even those about the humanity of Jesus and the mysteries of his life, so as to remain in pure emptiness and immersed in the divinity.[18] Teresa knew that one cannot identify Jesus with images and representations; nevertheless, she was convinced through her experience, as well as from Scripture and tradition, that we cannot at any point in the Christian life depart from the historical Christ, even less emphasize his divinity over his humanity. The risen Lord lives today. We find God in Jesus. There is no growth in Christian life apart from Jesus. The highest mystical marriage is with this Jesus-human. The human Jesus integrates our humanness. He entered our human condition completely and experienced human reality with all its brokenness, limitations, and weakness. Jesus prayed, struggled with God's will, and was fully human.

Now, to comment on the beauty of our Lord: there is no comparison, no lesser face or more attractive spouse than this jealous lover. I like the way Teresa talks about the inner thoughts. When we turn away from our Lord, we return the mind's eye back down deeply into that image in our soul, which is pervasive and ceaselessly available. She uses the word *Representar*, which is not an imaging but an affective movement of faith and love. This requires greater purity of heart. There is no place for the mind to land, as in thinking about thoughts, even if they are of Jesus! This is about consciousness: where the thoughts land, where the mind dwells, where the feelings rise, where the thinking mind cannot rationalize. Afflictions cost. Afflictions reduce the presence to a belief that is abstract and not a living presence. The remembering of God's mercy can remedy all inclinations toward afflictions or addictions. An affliction can be affections that are not well ordered. We love; our heart's desire is our Lord. Through the love of our Lord we love others. Teresa was called to unify her desires to one desire, our Lord.

This is what is dangerous about spiritual reading. It leads the thinking mind to dwell on speculative reasoning.

St. Teresa's practice of recollection is to return to that default of *Representar*. The Orthodox would use their icon of Jesus that is burned into their consciousness through the repetition of the Jesus Prayer.

Summary: We have studied two teachings that give us an imperative to shift from the consciousness that causes us to go away from God. The dynamic moral voice tells us clearly what to do, but the way into doing it is training of the mind. Let's look at St. Teresa's teaching on the practice of recollection: since God is within, we need to bring all thoughts toward God.

Practice of Recollection

We simply notice our thoughts rising in our mind. We gather them to one thought, the thought of the humanity of Jesus. We then focus toward Jesus and act as if he is here rather than as if he is not here. We bring our presence fully into the presence of our Lord. When I hear St. Teresa saying this in her teachings I can imagine her in the sixteenth-century monastery parlor engaged in lively dialogue with the visitor on the other side of the grill. What she taught her novices is to have Jesus as the "other" rather than anyone else.

We practice imaging our Lord as near rather than far away. Jesus is always looking at us, so the practice is with the mind's eye to look at him, or to feel the gaze that he is looking at us and we are in his sight. This is the practice of faith. Not faith as right belief in doctrine, but faith as a muscle that strengthens our resolve to follow our beliefs with our heart. There are two ways to practice this recollection: One is to empty our senses of everything else and to rein them in like we'd do with wild horses. The other is to focus and concentrate on Jesus as being right here, right now. St. Teresa talks about seeing Jesus over the shoulder of anyone we speak to. At first this might seem rude to the person with whom we are engaging in dialogue, but this is getting into the mystical realm where Jesus is really in that person anyway. We know what we are doing when we do it!

You might ask the question about vocation: is St. Teresa's affective disorder a conflict only because she was a nun? Can lay contemplatives place their affective energy toward God and count on God's grace to enable them to love their partners? Is this spiritualizing human emotions? Is this spirituality too high? Most current theology of marriage teaches to love one's partner and thereby love God. I'm suggesting that one loves God and God loves the spouse through the lay contemplative's well-ordered love. The more I listen to married persons and also gay and straight singles, the more I appreciate St. Teresa's teachings. All of us humans have a way out of our divided hearts: Jesus, our Lord. If we love him, he will become our teacher and source of grace to love others, whether they are our married partner, best friend, or sisters in a religious community. We love God with our whole heart, and then we love others as we love ourselves. This is the great commandment that liberates, gives life, and helps us selflessly serve others.

St. Teresa transcended that existential dread of loneliness through her wholehearted consecration to our Lord. This is the foundational myth of being a hermit. Literally being alone with the Alone was her vocation. As in all myths, there is a part of each of us that we can identify with that intense attraction of being alone, indeed being to Being. But that's a high state. Most of us are not ready for such radical renunciation. She recommended to her novices the practice of recollection that shifted their attention toward inner contemplation.

Recollection is a good place to start because Jesus becomes our teacher, friend, brother, spouse, confessor, healer, Lord. We might, however, be led to another practice that would be a good sequel to recollection: colloquy. If we had our inner dialogue with Christ Jesus instead of with ourselves, we would stay recollected and root out vainglory. Recollection roots out vainglory, but colloquy prevents those weeds from returning in our interior garden.

Recollection leads to the next practice that is helpful to root out the affliction of vainglory. A ceaseless prayer practice prevents the affliction of vainglory from rising in the thought patterns.

Praxis

Praxis of Colloquy: Dialogue with Our Lord

As I understand the unique disciplines of each practice, recollection is closer to mindfulness and being in the dimension of faith, whereas colloquy is a step further into the training of consciousness. Colloquy enables us to catch all that self talking to self and shift it to our Lord so that there is ceaseless thinking/talking interiorly to God rather than self talking to self. Impossible, you say? Actually, it is a natural progression to a deeper faith. If, in faith, Jesus is really present, then why should we act as if he is not really here, right here, right now? The problem is that we are in the habit of forgetting, or of thinking he doesn't care if we ignore him, or of thinking it is impossible to be so conscious of anything, let alone being conscious of God.

The solution is *praxis*. The training of the mind is necessary to shift this self-talk to talking/thinking/feeling toward God. What often stops the logic of this practice is a feeling that God really doesn't care that much about me. This must be rooted out as an attitude. He cares, cares very much, and will come into my heart if I want him to. He is shy and will not intrude. This mystery of free will is an absolute law that even God does not break into. Our autonomy, our zone of choice, is what it means to be other, so God respects this more than we do ourselves.

The *praxis* has three phases: First, we must invite our Lord into our innermost consciousness, mind, and heart. Second, we must start talking to him all the time about everything that we used to talk to ourselves about. And third, we must listen to his reply. His talk is through our subtle senses that might feel at first as if he is talking and we must practice faith to stay present to this very soft and gentle communication.

This colloquy is intermittent at first and is off and on. We literally forget God. Then, we simply return. Later, we forget ourselves and there is reduced "self-talk," so there is less talk even to God, but there is more walking in the presence of Christ in faith. This practice is not easy to learn. It takes strenuous effort at first. It takes many returns to keep it steady and conscious.[19]

This colloquy is appropriate for *lectio divina*'s many phases because our Lord brings to mind the text; then the study is not with the author but toward him. He shares all the levels of meditation and interacts with stories from the gospels and the Old Testament or other sources. He brings to mind which afflictions need to be rooted out so that purity of heart rises and the text can be seen as it was intended by the author. The full circle of *lectio divina* as prayer becomes real, conscious, and active.

Some people are suffering so much, however, that any training of the mind is simply too difficult. There is a practice that uses that suffering. It is the doctrine of the Little Way.

The *Praxis* of the Little Way: Our Teacher Is Thérèse of Lisieux (1873–97)

The Little Way is not just one more episodic way of praying; it is a whole new way of life that manages our suffering. We experience our weaknesses and shortfalls. We regret some of our actions and many of our rash judgments or ill wishes toward others. The trick is not to do self-correction or self-loathing but simply to notice how little we are and offer that very feeling to our Lord for the sake of someone else so that they can be healed or given strength for their journey. Our littleness is the content of this prayer in all its many forms. We notice and lift it up like we would say a Hail Mary or an Our Father. The emotional feeling is the prayer. We send it to our Lord and not back to ourselves, who can obsess on our woes.

This littleness becomes the content of prayer and the way is to simply offer it. These practices cannot be taught in abstraction, like a philosophical construct. It is only through practice and our experience that we actually "get it" and experience for ourselves how utterly simple it is and how much benefit is derived from such a consistent and ongoing practice. Also, to say this is not my way or to think of it as too childish might make us take another look: first of all, it is God, the director of our soul, that gives us our practice. We do not select the one suitable for us. And, second, we can only know it by doing it. These practices belong to the genre of wisdom literature that can only be grasped when the experience has already taken place. So we need simple, childlike faith that this is an invitation for us to enter into this Little Way as taught by St. Thérèse.

Her genius goes on to teach us more: all little acts of self-surrender can be used for substitutive suffering. We suffer and can use our suffering to substitute so that someone else does not have to suffer. We actually prevent suffering for someone else because we do it for them. In this exchange—all in faith lifting our heart toward the All-Merciful Love of Jesus who has redeemed us all—we join in his merits and in faith know that this actually heals and transforms others. Again, this is all faith and is steeped in the Christian biblical sensitivities of the nature of sacrifice having been fully satisfied by the cross and resurrection of Christ Jesus.

This doctrine, as St. Thérèse called it, was new. The former asceticism stressed external acts of penance and repetitive deeds. This stresses internal sufferings of the mind used as the words are used in prayer. Instead of praying words, St. Thérèse offered her suffering as prayer. Also, each act is more symbolic as an act of worship than an act of penance to remove the debris of sin or any quantifiable punishment equation.

This is the good news. Suffering has meaning and can be transmuted to help others. Our little saint, Thérèse, gives us concrete teachings. What is more exceptional is that she promises to come with her teachings. She is an embodied patron saint who is spending her heaven doing good through us. We no longer need to pick up a life of prayer and sacrifice; we use our ordinary emotions and ride our faith upon those flowers of intention.

There are story after story of conversions. Many priests and sinners attribute their new life of apostolic love to some connection with St. Thérèse. Her Little Way of using ordinary consciousness of feelings and relationships is prayer.

Now, lest this practice of the Little Way be construed as just one more theory about prayer, let me provide an example from life at Our Lady of Grace Monastery, my monastery here in Beech Grove:

As I understand the Little Way, it is to be used for little things that have an emotional valence. Here's the sequence: notice the irritation; lift it up; offer it to God's merciful love like Jesus' dying on the cross; offer it with an intention that says, "Take my suffering so that through your grace the person I'm offering for doesn't have to suffer. Substitute my little emotions (fuel for prayer) and relieve the harm, hurt, or danger from someone else."

Here are ten examples from this week:

1. When air conditioning is set too low and I feel chilled: offer for those suffering from climate disasters. I lift up my emotions around being cold and let those emotions be the prayer. I specifically make the intention for those suffering from flooding because of the storm.

2. When taking the stairs because the elevator is out of service again: offer the emotions of frustration because I have to climb four flights of stairs. I make an intention so I don't waste suffering: for the sake of my infirmed brother who has had a stroke and now lives in La Paz, Bolivia.

3. When remembering a duty that I must fulfill instead of making more progress on a given manuscript: I offer the regret of giving away my discretionary time and the frustration of a double workload for the sake of workers who have no discretionary time and have jobs they dislike or are ill-suited to do.

4. When hearing of a mother's frustration with children who no longer belong to any church: offer my feelings of helplessness and refrain from blame and commentary about our broken church for the sake of those children who need elders, teachings, and guidance.

5. When hearing a voice in choir off pitch and out of rhythm: offer the dissonance and my feelings of powerlessness and musical discomfort for those who are deaf or blind.

6. When feeling the harsh tone of political talk: offer the restlessness and disappointment about current leadership and voices of the media for those who have no rule of law in their land.

7. When sensing the worldliness of my conversations at table: offer my remorse for the sake of those who are leaving the table hungry for some words of encouragement and edification.

8. When reading my mail and getting a notice on health insurance policy: offer my bewilderment and ignorance for those who suffer alone and are in need of medical attention.

9. When reading an e-mail about an invitation that I'll decline: offer the crisis of limits for those who are ill and have no one to care for them.

10. When tempted to arrive late for prayers: offer my quick response to stop working and get to church on time for those who have no church to go to, or no faith in God, or no habit of prayer.

This list is infinite day by day and week by week. This becomes a way of living. Notice, respond in faith, and offer for the sake of another. This is redemptive suffering. We don't let any drop of blood coming from the side of our Lord to hit the ground.

There is no feeling too little or no intention too trivial to be left unsaid and to be used as the fuel for prayer and sacrifice. The Little Way is a practice that becomes prayer when made into one's way of life. Prayer is lifting up the heart to God. We can pray for others and actually help others through prayer by offering our sufferings to the redemptive power of Christ Jesus. We can use colloquy, the Jesus Prayer, or the Little Way as practices that become prayer.[20]

Personal Revelatory Text

An example of another person's sustained *lectio* might be helpful to see how each person has a particular encounter. For more than ten years Kathleen Cahalan and I have had lengthy conversations about sustained *lectio*. She is a professor at Saint John's University in Collegeville, Minnesota. My story with the book of Jonah is my *lectio* done as a nun in a monastery. I have asked Kathleen to share her story of *lectio* that she's done through her life as a wife, teacher, and scholar.

I underwent back surgery in 2005, and during the eight weeks of recovery I was allowed to sit for only twenty minutes a day, which included using the bathroom. The rest of the time I had to lie down, stand, or walk. I was already an avid walker and getting outside and moving around generally felt good. But as the days wore on I quickly succumbed to my greatest spiritual challenge: an overactive mind. When engaged in daily activities such as walking or lying on the sofa, my mind would plunge head first into free fall. Several years earlier my spiritual director, Sister Meg Funk, had taught me that early Christians who sought solitude in the desert were plagued by their thoughts and found it difficult to pray and concentrate. I could see that my thoughts tended to run all over the place, launching into stories, conversations, arguments, and full-fledged dramas in which I held center stage. So, the back surgery was one thing, but the inner afflictions were another thing that I was not expecting to be so rigorous. Some thoughts, as John Cassian (360–435 CE) notes, must be rooted out in order for God's word and presence to dwell within us.[21] *The practice is to attend to our thoughts as they rise and replace thoughts, especially afflictive thoughts, with the gospel text. The goal of this practice for Cassian is purity of heart; one seeks to cleanse the heart of all its desires in order to mold desire and the will toward God and away from self-centered thoughts. But when thoughts are afflictions of the self, there is no other text, reality, or space for another narrative. My afflictive thoughts tended to revolve around things, anger, and vainglory, and in that vortex the ego reigns supreme.*

Physical pain had brought me to a standstill. In the long recovery from the surgery (about nine months before I was pain free), I had not much energy for reading academic books or writing another paper. Rather, my free-fall thinking emerged as my dominant consciousness most of the time, and not only was I feeling trapped in a body I was not sure I was going to regain, but I was trapped in a world of thoughts that quite frankly made nighttime TV dramas seem bland. I was attacked by my inner tangles and webs. The body's vulnerability and the time it takes to heal became an invitation to me to return to a spiritual practice that had sustained me for a long time. But like most spiritual practice, I had to start over at the beginning. I had to enter back into the biblical text daily, to let the words and images sink into my consciousness and replace the loud speech and annoying static on the stream of my consciousness.

While lying on my back, I returned to reading the daily readings, a familiar practice since my childhood. I would try to memorize a line or phrase and carry it with me through the day, gently replacing my thoughts of anger or vainglory with the biblical text. This was especially helpful when I was out walking. I had another narrative that gradually eased out the violence of thoughts that came rushing in at me. The traditional form of lectio divina *involves the whole self: I do this method not in an hour but in days and weeks: the words begin on the lips (*lectio*), they rise to the mind (*meditatio*), they sink into the heart and a prayer rises to God (*oratio*), and the word emerges out into silence and rest in God's presence (*contemplatio*). The Scriptures, then, are scripted onto and into the body as well as the mind. One narrative replaces, or roots out, another narrative.*

After the initial eight weeks of home rest, I began intensive physical therapy, which included pool therapy, and I found significant pain relief from swimming. I discovered the healing quality of water, and for many months it was the only place I was pain free (in swimming aerobic style, with a waist belt, the spine is "unloaded" from all body weight and can be moved and strengthened without harm). I began swimming in the spring, and attended the Holy Week liturgies; at Holy Saturday I listened to the seven liturgical readings that recount the grand drama of salvation history. The fourth reading, from Isaiah 55, particularly spoke to me: "All you who thirst come to the water." I began to memorize that verse, starting one line at a time on my daily walks, and then more verses until I could recite the entire chapter. I had a cheat sheet, of course: I printed out the text and carried it with me on my walks so I could glance at the lines; as in any memorization, I had to take it one line at a time, until I could repeat it, and then add a second line and so on. When I went to the pool, I tried to repeat what I had memorized and I often could not remember or lost track of the next line or jumbled the lines together. Memorizing required intense concentration, more than I realized, and I had to work hard to make progress on both sets of exercises: the bodily movements and the movements of my lips and mind. It took several months before I could recite the entire text and only by repeated recitation could I keep it in and with me. I spent about eighteen months with Isaiah 55, and it reached a point where the text would come to me effortlessly when I woke in the morning, entered the pool, or went grocery shopping.

I had gone to the pool seeking physical relief and hopefully healing, though I had resolved myself to the reality that I might not be entirely pain free and would have to modify my life in terms of what I could do. I was surprised to find out that God was inviting me to another kind of healing. At first all I could think about was my bodily pain, but as I repeated the text on my lips, it began to form my consciousness and led me to another reality:

I had been immersed in the waters of baptism as an infant but I barely knew how to swim in those waters.

The opening verses of Isaiah 55 invite the thirsty and hungry to come to God's banquet, to receive wine, milk, and bread for no payment or cost (55:1-3). Spending money on what is not bread and what does not satisfy is emptiness, but Yahweh's "rich fare" is the true feast (55:2),[22] and like the Wisdom figure in Proverbs, Yahweh is luring us to a magnificent table (Prov 8). My problem was that I'd rather spend my money on new clothes, another book, or a computer upgrade. Didn't I deserve it? Or I'd rather "sit in the seat of scoffers" (Ps 1) and complain about how terrible my situation was. I had to spend all this time recovering, and for what? I could be doing something to make myself famous, like writing a book or giving a talk. If I didn't fully recover, I might have to give up parts of my professional life, travel, and becoming someone great. I might have to settle with staying home and just teaching.

The text ran deep. Here was God saying to me, "Come to the water" (55:1), "come to me heedfully, listen, that you may have life" (55:3). God had my attention: this time of recovery, painfully slow as it was, stopped me and invited me to look at my life: my ambitions, desires, and intentions. What I found quite honestly was a fairly driven, ego-dominant person who stood at the center of the world. Perhaps there was no other way for me to learn this lesson but by being brought low and made to stand still and swim gently in the water—at Gold's Gym, no less.

But what was I to listen to? The next few verses speak of God renewing the promises of the covenant, which meant for Isaiah's audience a return from exile. For me, it meant giving myself in total and complete trust to God's goodness and mercy and not worrying about my back, a full recovery, what meetings I was missing, or how I was going to live. All of that was not important, or not as important as sitting at the rich table set for me and listening to God. Perhaps the most powerful message lay in the next few verses:

> *Seek God while God may be found, call God while God is near. Let the scoundrel forsake his way, and the wicked woman her thoughts; Let them turn to the Lord for mercy; to our God, who is generous in forgiving. For my thoughts are not your thoughts, nor are your ways my ways, says the Lord. As high as the heavens are above the earth, so high are my ways above your ways and my thoughts above your thoughts. (Isa 55:6-9)*

My calling was actually quite simple: to seek God and nothing else. I had deliberately changed the text to be inclusive and that meant I had to say the words, "the wicked woman her thoughts." I had to renounce these thoughts of self, the vainglory that allowed me to do so much good for others so I would look good and be praised. I had to seek mercy and forgiveness for all my self-motivated driven-ness; I was not teaching, or writing, or living a life that was seeking God, but only for myself. And, of course, the following verses shouted to me: you are not God—not your thoughts or your ways. God's thoughts and ways are higher and unknown to you. I had to enter a pool of water, submit to daily exercises, to learn what I thought I knew as a trained theologian but clearly had never known.

After a long recuperation, I was healed from the grinding pain. In many ways I had my life back, but now it was a new life, for not only was I given my physical life back, but I

*experienced a new calling. What I didn't realize was that this
call was going to disrupt my life and teaching in significant
ways. But that is another story—one in which* lectio *continues
to play a crucial role.*

Kathleen's *lectio* began with experience. She was in
chronic back pain. She used the pain as prayer but soon
found nourishment in the immersion with the scriptural
texts. There was power and healing energies coursing
through her "putting on the word of God."

The whole event changed her. These prayer practices
do not in and of themselves save us. We still need help.
The virtue that guides the virtues is the art of discernment. Kathleen is now engaged in living a discerning
way of life because the word is so present. There's help
from the tradition to move to the next step: discernment.

All choices for action are to be made through the prism
of sorting out what takes us toward God, toward self, or
toward evil.

Discernment as Integral to the Moral Dimension of *Lectio Divina*[23]

The dynamic of discernment is the ultimate work of
this third dimension. The most important practice in this
third dimension of the moral voice heard by the personal
senses is the practice of discernment.

This manifestation of thoughts is the earliest form
of spiritual direction. We are transparent to our inner

inclinations; our thoughts become our indicators long before our behaviors act out our intentions. We notice the sources of our rising thoughts: from God, from self-centered desires, or from evil promptings. We notice the subtle graces that invite us to go toward God. To sort out these thoughts is called discernment (*diakrisis*).

This is the work of the monastery. The interior life of a contemplative is to do this interior discipline under the guidance of wise elders. We cannot exaggerate how important this middle way is to learn. Extremes are usually a sign of self-centeredness and extreme groups are a sign of madness. The teachings are clear (see *Conf.* 2.16).

We know that discernment is not a talent or an ability of our human faculties but a gift of the Holy Spirit (1 Cor 12). To discriminate toward God takes the grace of God to invite us, to incline us, to excite our heart toward our Creator. Not all are given the same gifts:

> To one is given through the Spirit the utterance of wisdom, and to another the utterance of knowledge according to the same Spirit, to another faith by the same Spirit, to another gifts of healing . . . to another the discernment of spirits. . . . All these are activated by the one and the same Spirit. (1 Cor 12:8-11)

The greatest gift we can receive is the gift of discernment because it helps us use all our gifts, talents, abilities, inclinations, and desires. Without this gift of discernment, we fail or sometimes go to extremes or follow our lowest desires and inclinations, either toward self or toward evil. We must seek this gift with all our strength and diligence.

Without the gift of discrimination—the ability to sort our thoughts and determine which are from God—we have no way for the mind to choose the good and follow after it. The law is planted in our heart, but the way to our heart is through the mind's eye that can detect which desires, thoughts, feelings, and images are toward our heart's desire, which is God.

How do we use the gift of discrimination in the real world? What does discernment look like as a method rather than a theory?

Discernment Is Sorting

To discern is to sort out, in the light of the whole, that which is of God. The goal of discerning is to reach purity of heart, a single point of light. Often we get caught up in a part and sometimes that single part becomes God or an idol.

The ascetical practices used by all the monastics in the desert were intended to reverse this tendency to make gods of ourselves or our things or events rather than let God be God in our lives. The condition we find ourselves in—ordinary consciousness—requires us to discern. This fog instead of a clear mirror is a result of the consequences stored in the teaching myth called original sin.

- We have a tendency toward evil.
- We are ignorant of the good.

- Or our will is weak even when we know what is good and attempt to strive against evil.
- We have that law printed in our heart but can't sustain acting on this impulse to do the loving thing. We forget.

This is our human condition, and it means that the work of discernment helps us know what is good, how to avoid evil, and how to be strong in our resolve to take refuge in Christ. We can do the loving thing. We can rely on the elders' experience from the desert tradition. Their teachings about the eight thoughts contain teachings about discernment at each thought.

Summary of the Eight Thoughts

We notice our thoughts. Usually a thought comes with a tail of little thoughts. If the first thought doesn't catch our attention, then the second or third one will. With the practice of watchfulness of thoughts, we can observe our thoughts and catch the moment we consent to the thought instead of letting it pass by. It's this consent that is our moment for choosing truth.

From the food thought we learn that fasting is a natural way to notice thoughts because it is easy to sense hunger. We can practice noticing the hunger thought, letting it pass by or consenting to it.

When we learn this, we learn the first step in discernment. In order to take the middle way, moderation is preferred:

- Not too much, not too little.
- Not too often, not too infrequent.
- Not too rich in quality, not too poor in quality.
- Extremes meet. It is risky to be on the edges. It's not recommended to eat too little, as it is not recommended to eat too much.

From the sex thought we learn that thoughts have a life of their own. We are not our thoughts, but we get hooked on them and they become a cycle. To break the cycle of thoughts, we should manifest them to a trusted elder.

The disciple practices humility, and the elder practices discernment and can often give a word to assist the discerning one.

We must not manifest our thoughts to just any older person. He or she should be beyond the afflictions themselves, at least beyond the predominant one that the disciple has trouble with. Even if there isn't an elder around, it is good to manifest thoughts, but the seeker is to disregard the example or advice of the elder if it is not in concert with the teachings from the desert tradition.

We must discern our sex thoughts at the first inkling before they cluster into feelings or passions. If we notice them soon, we can frequently redirect them swiftly. The goal is prayer and the abiding sense of God's presence rather than consciousness of food, sex, things, anger, etc. We strive to be the same in the night as we are in the day.

From the thing thought we see the value of refraining from analysis of thoughts except to sort through the source of the thought: self, God, or the devil. If the source is self, then appropriate remedies should be taken. If from God, then I need secure permission to use the things. If from evil, I must rid myself of the things and root out the attraction toward greed. Things also need the same discerning moderation: how many is more than I need; how many is too few? Having things too high or too low in quality also violates the spirit of using things as tools to mediate God. Too much time used in managing things snuffs out the spiritual life. The illusion of personal ownership needs to be rooted out. We are all cocreators using things as vessels of the altar.

From the anger thought we see the harm done to our ability to discern if we are afflicted with anger. We cannot see ourselves and are of no help to others when we are angry. We are blind. We cannot discern when we are angry, so anger must be entirely rooted out. Forgiveness can even anticipate anger.

The dejection thought teaches us to find the source of dejection. Is it from unresolved anger, harm done, dashed expectations, sin that fragments the mind and divides the heart? Or is it chemical? Treatment depends on the cause. If from sin, confess. If depression is from unresolved anger, forgive. If our thoughts are from unknown origins, compassion is required. If the source is exaggerated self-esteem, then humility is the remedy.

From the *acedia* thought we learn that we are not the best judges of ourselves. When we are bored and tempted to abandon the spiritual journey, we need to stay in our cells, return to the routine of the monastic life, and do manual labor. We need to cultivate compunction. We desire truth, which is humility. Work becomes prayer, and prayer and work are interchangeable.

From the vainglory thought we learn how to discern whether we are being self-centered rather than selfless. We understand that we must refrain from daydreams and fantasies where we are the center of attention. We learn that our motivation (our thought about the thought) matters. We learn that we can do all the right things for the wrong reasons.

Discernment helps us factor out our second thoughts, that is, our intentions. These must be sorted too: is our intention from God, from self-interest, or from evil inclinations? When motivations are true, the monastery can be the world and the cell is our heart.

From the pride thought we learn the steps of humility—to align our thoughts, words, and deeds with truth. In pride, we see the results of thoughts that have origins rooted in evil. If their source is from evil spirits, we need to be alert.

Evil spirits do exist and to deny the force of evil entities is a weapon used to confuse the victim of evil (*Conf.* 8.2.1). Cassian says we have two spirits, one our guardian angel and the other a demon trying to snatch our souls (*Conf.* 8:17.1).

Demons cannot read our thoughts but can see our outward demeanor and tempt us according to what they perceive as our weakness. There are many varieties of evil beings, some more harmful than others. Some are neutral. They seem to specialize in certain areas of concentration related to the eight afflictions.

Sources of the Afflictions

Afflictions can have two sources: one is our inner disposition and the other could come from without, evil spirits. We need to have a healthy regard for evil entities that have intelligence as their destructive power.

Our Inner Dispositions

Our inner dispositions can cause us to go up the chain of leading a self-centered life. The ego is an illusion. We tend to accept promptings of false quests for happiness that are short-sighted or harmful to others. The teachings on the eight thoughts have a sturdy description of these pitfalls. I recommend a study of the affliction of carnal pride for that teaching. What is not taught today is a realistic view of spiritual pride that is caused by evil spirits that are entities.

Subtle Forces of Evil[24]

Evil entities have higher intelligence than humans and can enter our body and even our mind without our consent. While they can disturb our minds with confusion and even possession, they cannot take over our soul unless we consent.

This is why we must be vigilant and know ourselves, know when we consent and when we refuse temptation and cancel the attraction. Demons are of varying degrees of evil. Most of the time they do not seem evil but come in the form of light, either as a good that is not God or an apparent good that wins our affections.

What do these embodied spirits look like? Evil entities are creatures with subtle bodies (particles) and with consciousness and intelligence. They come in differing forms for their dark work in the world. The personification of evil with names of entities is simplistic and has the effect of taking away from the fact that there are many, many domains between us and our creator God.

The Scriptures contain the names of animals given to a variety of devils to indicate the range of their cunning, haunting, attractive, repulsive, or magical appearances. Evil entities are both light and dark. Some come through doors, make noises, and incite negative feelings. Other evil entities are sweet, friendly, give counsel and the confidence to perform spiritual feats.

We repel evil entities by blessed objects: holy water, a crucifix, medals, and candles. These are forces that through faith in Christ can be used against evil. The prayer taught by our Lord, the Our Father, has a depth and power equal to any evil in our fragile world.

Most evil forces are held in check by ordinary faith and practice.[25] We take refuge in Christ Jesus and our Christian way of life repels these dark forces. But all of us must be vigilant.

It seems that purity of heart is required for a minister to cast out demons. Like the sacrament of reconciliation it's not hard to do the ritual. What is difficult is to free up the one who is infected.

It might be helpful to review some basic teachings on this subject of evil.

The first level of evil that could beguile us from our inner self or from an outside entity (demon) is called a temptation. It could be minor or major, but it uses the cycle of urges to move the person or a group into taking action and even making the evil actions a habit. This is ordinary evil that happens to all of us over and over again. Most of the teachings of the desert elders are to deal with this kind of ordinary evil.

The second level gets into the extraordinary activities of outside forces that invite us to evil activity: (1) infestation, (2) oppression, (3) obsession, and (4) possession.

The first demonic activity is infestation, which pertains to objects or locations. This is a manifestation of weird objects not being where they were placed, or chilling winds, or blood spots appearing on walls. The varieties baffle ordinary consciousness. An exorcist can pray the evil out of these places, using holy water, the crucifix, and sacramentals (holy objects). The persons who dwell there also must participate in the prayers through their faith and willingness to have their things healed. The causes are as many as the symptoms. It could have been cursed, there might be harmful activity in that location that still has a residue. But infestation can be removed by prayer, and the place or object can be holy where it was once a source of consternation.

The second level of evil is oppression, sometimes called "physical attack." This shows itself by the marks of physical blows on the victim's body. People literally are physically attacked by an evil entity. This harm can be healed and prevented from any reoccurrence through a skillful exorcist through prayer and courageous faith.

The third level is obsession. This level is when the devil is the tempter. An entity actually attacks the victim with persistent, intense suggestions to the mind that torment like a fixation. It could be in ordinary consciousness or in nighttime dreams. The blur here is to separate this experience from mental illness. It could be a form of schizophrenia, or it could be both a demonic attack from an entity and also caused by one's mental illness. I asked Fr. Jack Ryan, the former exorcist of the Archdiocese of Indianapolis, how he could tell the difference and he said if it is from the devil (evil entity) then spiritual objects such as holy water and the Eucharist would cure the victim. It might take many sessions to eject the evil one, but it is well worth it, especially if the person is already mentally troubled; he or she does not deserve the Evil One too.

The fourth level is possession. This is involuntary on the victim's part and the evil entity actually goes inside and takes over one's speech, body movements, etc. Most of the time the person goes into an unconscious state and will not remember what happens, but sometimes they are aware. It is a dreadful affliction that takes many, many sessions of the exorcist. It also takes a faith community that prays and fasts during the long siege that could last for years. To people possessed by demons, these combats with intelligence are not strange or spooky. The demons become companions, are familiar, feed a need for being something special, and even flirt with risk in the lives of the possessed. A strange affinity toward evil develops.

To do what is necessary to expel them goes against their inclination because of a bond, an attachment, even a mingling of attitudes, goals, and mission. These people can "cast" these demons toward others as a weapon and so become quite strong in using spiritual forces.

Again, remembering a conversation with Fr. Ryan, the Evil One is not to be feared. Jesus Christ is so much more powerful and can outwit the Evil One from our realms. He also said that 99 percent of the time when he talks to victims of evil there is a natural cause that provided a portal for the Evil One. He said those most at risk are people who play with Ouija boards or black magic games, dabble in occult rituals, curse others or are cursed by others using the name of Satan, frequent evil places or people, or use things that flirt with calling down spirits and ancestors. All this can be harmful.

When I heard this I found a new zeal to use the Jesus Prayer, to have the name of Jesus in my heart. This protects me from evil influences. But "Fear not" is said 366 times in our Christian Scriptures.

In discernment, we sort out our thoughts to see if they are of God. God's way is toward peace. When we go God's way, consolation is the fruit. We can expect happiness.

Benefits are bountiful and beyond expectations. Even the body feels lighter and moves more and more to subtle feelings, emotions, and an abiding disposition of wonder. God will not give us any affliction beyond our capacity.

Our energy naturally flows toward others. We feel that our intellectual powers are sharper. We understand Scripture. Our experience seems congruent with our expectations. Our memory improves. Equanimity replaces anxiety and worry. Our eyes are clear, and we are helpful to others.

We gradually find that sorting thoughts becomes easier and more natural. The grace to go toward God feels better than making choices for the self. Evil is repulsive, but we know ourselves well and we continuously practice ceaseless repentance. Here, we know the safe harbor of compunction.

How can we know if our thoughts are from the self? If the source of the thought is from the self, we can notice a resistance or attraction that is thick with affect. When we are acting from the self, we have amazing energy and feed on the benefits. The affliction of anger, especially, makes us feel righteously powerful.

The self has subtle, even cunning, punishments attached if we give in to it. I tell myself I'll get mad, depressed, anxious, or sick if I don't get my way about this. So the "self way" sets up conditions for happiness. We even teach others how to gratify us! We coach; we ask for this or that praise.

We feed into another's need to please us. We look good but do the right thing for the wrong reason. Life becomes all about my needs, my wants, my desires, and my ambitions.

The self wants to be rewarded for being good and feels unjustly blamed if criticized, regardless of wrongdoing on the part of the self. Is there a way out of the self? Yes: discernment. We sort our thoughts and make choices to consent to God's way.

Discernment in the Monastic Tradition

Discernment is the technical word for training our thoughts. The word *diakrisis* means to sort thoughts, see their source, and see how they lure us into one of the eight afflictions.

To discern is to reason. It is part of the work of the second renunciation—making decisions that will enable us to follow our commitment to purity of heart. Discernment is also part of the work of the first renunciation, aligning our exterior life with our interior life of virtue and fulfilling our baptismal promises. There is an urgency today to use discernment in making major decisions: vocational choices such as ordination to priesthood, final vows, marriage, or divorce.

If we have a major decision to make, the following process will be helpful. Notice our thoughts. Watch them rise and fall. Be aware how in any given day our thoughts and emotions shift, change, and go full circle. Do not be quick to act, since thoughts are fickle. We are not our thoughts. They come and they go. How can we trust them? Where are they from? Are the thoughts from God, self, others, or evil entities?

First, we seek God's help in the matter before us. We take the decision at hand to prayer, in the name of Jesus Christ or the Holy Spirit. The Our Father is the classic prayer that teaches us to ask for what we need. Prayer before, during, and after discernment is essential. In humble supplication, we ask God not only for the wisdom to make the right choice but also for the grace to carry it out. We know in advance that God's way is the most beneficial for all concerned. Sorting is simply to remove oneself so that God's presence can spring up.

This process does not lead to quietism. It is hard work to sort, to receive, to be willing to see truth, and to do whatever it takes to follow the impulses of grace. Even though God can accomplish anything in a flash, the traditional steps are not arbitrary. They follow an orderly progression.

We know that the decision is in one sense already made, since the answer is deep inside us. Our body, mind, and soul know what's best for us at this time. We only need to bring it to consciousness, sort through the options, and find the energy (grace) of the moment.

Seven-Step Process.[26]

1. Pray for enlightenment
2. Sort our thoughts
3. Virtually live into the decision
4. Look for a confirming sign

5. Make the decision
6. Ritualize the decision
7. Guard our heart and watch our thoughts

Let's look at these steps one by one.

Pray for enlightenment: St. Benedict says that whenever we begin any good work, we should beg earnestly in prayer for guidance about the right action and for the ability to carry out the consent. Here's where a pattern of prayer is the key ingredient.

If we pray only when we have a major choice or a divide in the road, we will have a hard time praying at the moment of discernment. There are hints and road signs along life's way, but what makes our life a way to God is having a practice of prayer. With training, we can sense the impulses of grace and have already in place a willingness to follow God's call.

Sort our thoughts: We watch our thoughts as they rise and fall, sorting them into three buckets—toward self, toward God, and toward evil. We notice which thoughts weigh most heavily on our mind, and eventually we see a pattern arise.

Virtually live into the decision: We make a hypothetical decision based on the sorting in step 2.

We take that tentative choice through the sorting process once again: is it toward self, toward God, or toward evil? We notice what this choice says.

If possible, we manifest our thoughts to a wise elder. We simply lay out the thoughts, just as they seem to us.

We do not gather more data. We try to verify whether indeed this choice that seems to be emerging is God's way for us.

If the hypothetical choice still seems viable, we move to the third step. We take the decision as a tentative given and test it. We put it on and act as if it is a decision that is final and to be implemented. Do we feel good about it? Usually if it is God's way, we feel a profound joy. Even if the decision has difficult consequences, the grace seems to be there to live with it.

Then, we keep it in our mind as if the decision has been made, for at least two weeks—long enough to have several moods and to watch how we handle the climate of this decision.

During this third step we may listen to other opinions and gather data but always consider that data in the light of the tentative decision. The reason not to invest too much weight on the feedback of others is because they are telling us what they would do.

Their advice is coming through their thoughts. What they would do, however, may or may not be helpful to us. To live this as if it were real, we talk within ourselves about the as-if decision. It is best not to tell others that you've made the decision because they will then make the decision a fact, and we will end up managing their grief or delight instead of knowing our thoughts.

We continue to live the two weeks (or another prudent space of time) as if we were implementing the tentative decision.

Look for a confirming sign: We look for a sign from God that is convincing and supportive of the decision. We check our feelings and see if they are joyful and peace-filled. Even hard things should have a grace to match the difficulty.

If there is no confirming sign, no consolation, or no ability to live in the decision as if it were real, then it is best to go back to step 1, take up another as-if decision, and see if we have more confidence in an alternative option.

But if the as if brings joy and there's grace to do it and the confirming sign brings peace, then the decision is probably right.

Make the decision: We make the decision, putting it in concrete terms. I've decided to _____ (whatever the decision is). The decision is most helpful when it is clear and action-oriented and when I am the subject, the doer. Even if the decision is passive—"I will not do X"—it is defining, with boundaries for implementation.

A decision requires the will to act. It represents a deliberate choice. It is one of the most awesome things a human can do: make choices and follow through as a cocreator with God. Notice that the decision isn't a goal or an aspiration but a deed to be done and done by me.

Ritualize the decision: Perhaps we light a candle, or write a letter confirming it, or call a friend. Mark the day on your calendar. Do the first step to implement it. In a sense, once the decision is made, all is already done—only not yet!

Guard our heart and watch our thoughts: Do what was envisioned. There's more to implementation than doing the work.

Doing it includes the interior work of guarding our heart and watching our thoughts. This takes a lifetime. While implementing the decision, from time to time there will arise the thought that I wished I had not done X. At the earliest notice of that thought dash it against the rock that is Christ. We already know the value of guard of the heart and watchfulness of thoughts. Therefore, we consider our decision final and all "what ifs" as simply temptations to divide our heart and fragment our mind. We return to our ceaseless prayer.

You may say, "But what if I did make the wrong decision?" You made it in good faith and in prayer. If you should go now in another direction, God will make that evident in a significant way, so for the daily work of implementing this decision you need only attend to carrying out your resolve.

This pattern of living a discerned life is the work of all of us no matter what exterior form it may take. We should be at peace because we made the decision in good faith and God will show us a major sign if we are to change our decision.

Our goal is purity of heart, lining up our external life so that it expresses our intentions to seek God in everyone and everything all the days of our life. Let me lay out a scenario that may be helpful in situations that require this discernment process.

Examples of Discernment from Life

EXAMPLE 1

Question for Discernment

Should I undergo extensive treatment for cancer? Yes, I am willing to do it! Is this God's will for me?

Step 1: Pray and Fast

Call on the Holy Spirit for guidance, light, and warmth.

I have been diagnosed with cancer. The doctors recommend extensive chemotherapy, followed by radiation treatments. "O Lord, come to my assistance; O God make haste to help me!" Spend time in prayer and turn completely to God and ask for guidance to go God's way.

Step 2: I Sort My Thoughts

Toward self: If I do the cancer treatments and they are effective, this would mean more years in this life, time to reconcile with foes, time off work, pain-free living and quality of life, more time with friends and community, etc.

Toward evil: It would let me get me what I deserve. I've worked for health benefits, and they might as well serve me rather than others; I have a lot of fight in me and need to get even for some of the hurts people have inflicted on me.

Toward God: I could increase my practices. I could endure the suffering for the sake of others. I could undergo extreme treatments and contribute to science. I could give up goals, start over, and set realistic objectives for the sake of my community; maybe I could put my personal goals into a secondary position for the sake of others.

Step 3: I Make a Decision to Live Virtually

I will do this virtual phase for three days. I gather data, but in my thoughts I act as if I have made the decision to undergo treatment to see if the decision holds up. I'll start the program in July. I sort my thoughts again, while living as if I am in rigorous cancer treatment.

Toward self: This is good for me to identify with other women who live with cancer and for me to face my mortality with courage and some defiance.

Toward God: With more time to live on this earth I have a chance, at the age of seventy, to start over with more mature values. I will make community primary and budget time for assigned work—prayer, reading, and some involvement with a group of like-minded souls.

Toward evil: I'll show everybody how tough I am. I can also take downtime whenever I feel like it and call it sick days. I'll do those things for myself that I've always wanted to do, no matter how it might interfere with community obligations.

Step 4: I Look for a Confirming Sign

This sign should be definitive, compelling, from God, and toward the good that the decision will effect. I should notice a good, peace-filled feeling. Even if part of the treatment would be difficult, there's an abiding grace that enables me to do tough things.

This is also the time I consult more people and gather more data. I let all thoughts come and do inner work measured against the virtual decision. It is necessary for me to stay with the virtual decision because if I keep switching back and forth, my thoughts cannot go deep and the decision can't rise in a solid manner.

I'll ask my confidante to hear out my thinking on this: I'll call my spiritual director and get some quality time with her and see if she thinks I am doing the right thing.

If the sorting of thoughts points to either selfishness or evil; if I can't live in the two weeks of virtual reality of implementing the decision; if there is no confirming sign; if there is no joy, peace, or consolation; if there's a vague discomfort and an abiding restlessness; if there's an anxiety that's deep and abiding—then return to step 1 and make an alternate decision.

Second alternative virtual phase: If there was no confirming sign that I should undergo the treatment, I'll take two weeks to pray into and sort out how it feels if I take the other direction of not undergoing the treatment for cancer and letting my body move toward health or toward death, if that be God's will.

Second round of sorting thoughts: The decision is at hand. Should I decline the option of treatment for cancer? Virtually live the consequence for two days.

Toward self: It would be easier just to live my life as best I can rather than treat the disease and do the intense medical tests and have anxiety about all the blood counts, etc. It would be less costly for the community. I could concentrate on doing what I can with the time I have left. I can skip all those little decisions about which treatment and when. I can request pain management. I can face life and death equally without so much effort to live for the long haul. I can cut my losses and say I've tried enough for this lifetime.

Toward evil: I have no hope in doctors. I don't deserve to live longer; I just might make a bigger mess of my life. The community would be better without me. I can at least shorten my life if I can't end it myself. I have the right to determine my own death.

Toward God: I have faith that the next life is more explicitly with God and have lived this life as well as I could have under the circumstances. I count on God's mercy. Brother Lawrence wrote in his Fifteenth Letter, "I have been near death several times and have never been so content as then; and so I did not ask for relief but rather for the strength to suffer courageously, humbly, and lovingly."[27]

If the sorting of thoughts points to either selfishness or evil; if I can't live in the two weeks of virtual reality of implementing the decision; if there is no confirming sign; if there is no joy, peace, or consolation; if there's a vague discomfort and an abiding restlessness; if there's an anxiety that's deep and abiding; if there is still no confirming sign, go into a third discernment—then look for the middle way between extremes.

Return to step 1. Should I take the first step and do at least one round of treatment? Then follow the steps above, again. When there is a confirming sign move to the decision.

Confirming sign:

- an event or experience that places the decision as if it is already happening
- other options are very far away from the confirmed option, no second best
- is unexpected and comes from beyond the people making the decision
- takes into consideration all the concerns and shows the way forward
- could not be contrived or set or engineered by human ingenuity; it has the feeling of a blessing, of God

Step 5: Make the Decision

I will undergo a first round of treatment for the next three months.

Step 6: Ritualize the Decision

We invite friends to share the decision, offer a special prayer, and celebrate the decision.

Step 7: Implement the Decision and Guard the Heart and Watch the Thoughts against Temptations

Make plans to move toward the initial treatment. Then, if I have second thoughts, I guard my heart and watch my thoughts. Every time a thought or a challenge emerges from the unconscious or from an outside source about the decision, I dash it against the rock that is Christ.

It is just a temptation. For example: I will not take treatment for three months and see how I am. If I still need treatment and it is available, I'll start then but not now. This is not an option. Through prayer and sincerity, the decision was made to do immediately the three months of treatment. That should be honored. If, for some reason, it is not available or it can't be helpful to my condition, then that determines my action, but I no longer need to second-guess my original faith-felt, honest deliberation.

There is great peace when discernment is at work and God is in charge of how it all works out. Peace of mind is a gift of well-ordered decisions made in the light of the Holy Spirit.

EXAMPLE 2

Question for Discernment

Should I seek permission to become a hermit? Yes, I'll do it! Is this God's will for me?

Step 1: Pray and Fast

Call on the Holy Spirit for guidance, light, and warmth. I am in transition. If I am ever going to do it, the time is now. I have been heading in this direction for some years, maybe all my adult life. "O Lord, come to my assistance, O God, make haste to help me!" I will make a special holy hour every evening for two weeks and ask God for guidance to go further toward our Lord.

Step 2: I Sort My Thoughts

Toward self: If I get to be apart, I can be more with myself and get my practices in a routine with fewer interruptions. I can get rested from all these years of overwork.

I can begin a more disciplined routine of my day with study, physical exercise, balanced diet, and well-ordered relationships. I need to stop, rest, and take care of myself. No one can do that for me.

Toward evil: I no longer believe in the values of my community as they are currently lived. I no longer benefit from the way the monastic life is lived here. I need to start my own monastic life, at least with myself. I have been a contributor long enough and now will let the community sponsor me. They have never let me do what I want and I do not care if my absence is a hardship on my community. They deserve to suffer a little.

Toward God: I accept the invitation for more time with our Lord. I am ready to take up this alone way of life to get ready for my dying process. I know the demons come with me into the silence, the cave, the cabin in the woods. I know it will be most difficult, but I count on God's mercy. Of myself, I could never do this. I've hungered to do this protracted silence so that I can be more careful about teaching ahead of my practice.

Step 3: I Make a Decision to Live Virtually

Before I ask my superior if I can live as a hermit for one year, I had better practice in my heart to see if I can do it. For my own discernment, I'll try to live as a hermit for a week to ten days virtually, that is, as if I am a hermit. If I succeed, I'll make an appointment with my superior to ask for time to discern with her. The point is to stay with the virtual decision to sink deeply into the consequences.

I gather data, but in my thoughts I act as if I have made a decision to become a hermit. I watch and see if the decision holds up and is firm. "I'll start today living as if I am already a hermit." Then I sort my thoughts.

Toward self: I'm finally getting the rest that I've needed for years. I am exhausted living with all those people. Their agenda was getting to me. I am off the strenuous schedule. I can cook food that I prefer and eat as I feel necessary. I am just so tired of the routine. It is a relief to slow down and gather my energy for the next thing.

Toward evil: I'm never going back into that tight living in the monastery again. I prefer to hold back my talent even if I have to return. They do not deserve my time and gifts anymore. I've done my part. Let them suffer without me. I actually hope the place falls apart. They deserve to suffer. I am sure living alone should have some moments of compensation. I've paid my dues. I am not going to be accountable. My weekly check-in will just be about the weather. No one has a right to my soul. I will live these first weeks just getting relaxed and rested and figure out my *horarium* in a few months. I might even take a few excursions, since I've saved some money and gotten some gifts. I'll . . .

Toward God: I am finally now a hermit. I must anticipate my afflictions that come with me. I have so much anger about my health, my lack of diligence. I will pray harder not only for guidance but for stability of emotions to sustain my resolve and to follow the *horarium* blessed by my superior. I need to follow closely my rule of life that is fitting for being a hermit.

So, I act as if I am a hermit for about two weeks; this is interior and not shared with anyone except my superior and/or spiritual director. I do little things as if I were a hermit: separate my things, sort them out. Pack a box of necessary things that I'd take with me. Make a list of things I need and sort out what I won't take with me. I enter into sleep and awake in the virtual reality.

I do inner mock days: wake up, pray alone, eat alone, walk alone, do *lectio*/Office/study/food preparation/handiwork alone for one day, two days, three days. See if I can stabilize my thoughts and stay in the virtual reality of being a hermit.

Step 4: I Look for a Confirming Sign

This sign should be definitive, compelling, from God, and toward the good that the decision will effect. I should notice a good, peace-filled feeling. Even if the decision is difficult there should also be an abiding strength to carry out the decision.

Confirming sign:

- an event or experience that places the decision as if it is already happening
- other options are very far away from the confirmed option, no second best
- is unexpected and comes from beyond the people making the decision

- takes into consideration all the concerns and shows the way forward
- could not be contrived or set or engineered by human ingenuity; it has the feeling of a blessing, of God

Examples of a confirming sign: A major obstacle is removed. A health issue is resolved or a barrier is overcome, for example, a new member steps up and takes over one's obligations. The superior takes initiative and calls for sisters to consider the opportunity as the hermitage is open and ready, etc. (If I cannot stay virtually as a hermit and if there is no confirming sign, redo the virtual decision using the opposite choice: live as if I'll not be a hermit and refrain from asking permission. Take the topic off the table and return to step 3.)

Step 5: Make the Decision
The decision is made to become a hermit first for six weeks, then to be assessed.

Step 6: Ritualize the Decision
We invite friends to share the decision, offer a special prayer, and celebrate the decision.

Step 7: Implement the Decision and Guard the Heart and Watch the Thoughts against Temptations
You made the decision in good faith and God received the resolve. If it is to change, it will come from the outside and not from inner ambivalence. It is the evil one working against the good that the decision will affect.

We need not only teachers to show us a method for discerned actions but also spiritual directors who care and care enough to journey with us at such important junctures of our life. We can find people who would tell us what they would do or they would encourage us to go for it, but what we need is to find—as in "discover"—God's way for us.

Spiritual Direction and Discernment

From the desert tradition we learn that the earliest form of spiritual direction was manifestation of thoughts to a wise elder. In the monastic tradition these elders responded with a word from Scripture. The sacrament of confession replaced the disclosure of thoughts to a wise elder. This happened in part because the tradition about the thoughts and how to practice vigilance through guard of the heart and watchfulness of thoughts got lost, mostly because attention was shifted to above the river about work or common monastic observances, such as chanting for hours and hours a day in choir. The other factor was the lack of wise elders, and priests became functionaries who gave absolution in the sacrament that was prescribed by the church.

To link the beautiful practice of disclosure to a wise elder, we need to train the wise elders into the role so that the practice can come full circle. Who qualifies as an elder?

There were conferences in the monastic tradition speaking about the teachings, compiling them into rules. For us who live in the third millennium, we can access these teachings only through prayerful reading or by doing *lectio divina* on these inspired texts. But, you might say, is not there anyone with whom I can talk? How can I do the practice of manifestation of thoughts as the early monastics did?

We all feel the need of a wise elder who can act as our spiritual director. Our inclination is part of surrendering to God. It is also good for us to trust and entrust ourselves to someone else in a visible manner. The joy of being heard is blessing and a sheer gift.

From the view of the listener, the director: Be welcoming and listen. Let the thoughts of the seeker come and refrain from engaging in conversation. Perhaps the seeker will need a few clarifying words to shift him or her away from commentary on those thoughts.

Encourage only straight talk. Refrain from problem solving. Let the words flow, session after session. Listen for which affliction is operative.

At some point, when the seeker seems ready, ask questions about how he or she is attempting to deal with the affliction. Then offer the teaching about the affliction and a practice or tool to help the person control that affliction.

Then, session after session, listen to how the practice is going. Lead them into doing *lectio* with a spiritual classic that teaches that practice, for example, *He and I* for colloquy practice, or *The Cloud of Unknowing* practice.[28] The listener teaches the theory behind the practice and helps the seeker remove any obstacles to the practice and develop a positive way to use the tool, for example, setting up a "cell" at home. The listener accepts the sacred trust of confidence and promises to pray for the seeker.

The best preparation for the listener is *lectio divina* and personal practice, using the tools as needed. The spiritual director, as we see from the desert tradition, is a tool herself, a tool for the training. When we need someone like this, God provides. If the student is ready the teacher appears.

From the point of view of a seeker, the selection of an elder requires finding someone who doesn't have the same afflictions or, if she had them at one time, now uses tools to keep them before God's mercy. The process of manifesting thoughts is simply to say what comes to mind. Name the obstacles to prayer, simply and humbly. If possible, refrain from analysis and commentary. Just let the words flow and notice the thoughts. Take the time required to slow down your thoughts. Shift down a gear in order to see one thought at a time. If you are confused about which thoughts are from God, self, or evil, ask your elder.

If you are stuck in a loop of circular thinking, lay each thought out as if you were shaking flour from your hands. Share your thoughts about motivations and intentions. If you have secrets, test them by sharing them. It's not the content of the secret that is important as much as it is the nature of secrets to control thoughts and escalate into dramas. Clarify questions about practice. Share insights from *lectio*. Begin with prayer and end with a blessing.

A wise elder facilitates a discerning heart and receives the soul seeking God. The qualification to be a wise elder is not a degree in spirituality or a certification in spiritual direction but humility. Humility is what people see of purity of heart. Staying humble is a process of discernment. The one undergoing purification, even if illumined, would require watchfulness, vigilance, being ever aware of God's presence. The credentials for a spiritual director are to be beyond the grip of afflictions and to have a continuous interior life of disciplined asceticism. To teach the contemplative way of life, one must have the interior discipline of doing the practices. The subtle risings of the Holy Spirit are met by the supple soul. The director is neither too lax nor too rigid. We must have discrimination to know the sources of our thoughts and the willingness to follow the promptings that come from God.

A wise elder can detect what is right effort. I remember the Dalai Lama saying to us at Gethsemani in 1996 that what separates Christians and Buddhists is the notion of effort.

Buddhists see self-effort as right practice, and Christians see that God's grace directs their effort. Therefore, we must discern, or sort out, what God wants of us, what the way of grace is inviting us to follow. We find God's will in the rising of thoughts that are sourced in God rather than sourced in ourselves or in evil. Watching our thoughts and laying them out in disclosure can help us see the impulses of grace made manifest. A wise elder can confirm our choices before we act.

The Wise Elder's Assistance

A wise elder can assist us to see the earliest phase of our thoughts. Sorting our thoughts detects not only sources (God, self, or evil) but the thought itself from the subtlest stirring to the stage of passion. Let's look again at the cycle of how thoughts rise from mere inkling to total habit.

The earliest detection is the easiest to redirect. The sequence moves from happening to the thinker to consent and even to captivity. To sort out these thoughts is called discernment (*diakrisis*). The term "discernment of spirits" (*diakrisis ton pneumaton*) is what Paul talks about in 1 Corinthians 12:10. It's one among many of the gifts that include wisdom, knowledge, faith, healing, mighty deeds, prophecy, speaking languages, interpreting languages. The discernment of spirits sorts out the source, authenticity, and degree of intensity and seriousness of spirits.

The practitioner is to mistrust his or her impressions that form judgments. We are invited to test the spirits (*dokimazete*) to see if they are from God (1 John 4:1). It's God's judgment (*ton karion*) that is for our good.

We look at them and weigh them against what we know to be true, whole, and companions to our commitment and what seems counterfeit or tricks that steal into our field of memory or judgment.

We manifest our thoughts to prevent the closed circuit of patterns that obscure prayerful discernment and full-bodied consent to responsible actions. We cannot judge from inside because we are the very ones in the dark of "I don't know." The best person who can see the light is one on the other side of the afflictions. We are in the midst of our darkness so we manifest our thoughts to a wise elder.

To avoid what is unpleasant and to do what is sweet isn't enough for complexity to provide insight. "Desolation" and "consolation" are technical terms to describe major emotional programs that provide helpful guidance. Again, given the prism of our ignorance, propensity toward sin, and weak strength of resolve (will), we need an outside view and encouragement from another.

Discernment is to sort and then to consent to the good and act accordingly. Discernment starts with the thoughts, not the will. We must know our thoughts so we can be willing to follow the subtle impulses of grace. The will is gentle and strong at the same time when the grace is abundant and clear. Grace is a word for easy, soft, natural, and attractive. God's way is always possible and is our heart's desire. It's also a whole way of life, not just for major decisions of vocation or location.

The more we act and walk God's way and refrain from the chains of our afflictions, the more we understand God's way and the sweeter life and all its living is.

Sequence of Thought

Again, notice the sequence of our thoughts: Besides knowing both our thoughts and the sources of those thoughts, there's the ever-constant noticing of the rising of thoughts earlier and earlier and even anticipating them.

- The first stage is a vague concept or feeling without even a concept structured to name it anything.
- The second stage is an image, or pre-phantasm, that has a feel.
- The third stage is a quality of solidity: maybe a thing, a memory, or an "is-ness."
- The fourth stage is an invitation that couples the "I" or "me" to the thought or feeling.
- The fifth stage is a dialogue of "what if–ness" that entices the invitation to action with some rationale and motivation.
- The sixth stage is the question: the yes-or-no proposition ends with consent or refusal.
- The seventh stage is to follow the consent with action and intent.
- The eighth step is to repeat the action and solidify the motivation.
- The ninth step is to couple the action/intention with identity. This is who I am, I say to myself.

Discernment is to back the thought/feeling to its early stages and notice them and make appropriate choices or consent.

The Burden of the Law and the Freedom of the Spirit

The emphasis on the will—about patterns of consenting or refusing actions that are in keeping with one's commitments (vocation)—is a later tradition of law-and-order methods. To isolate the will as a faculty of choice is the teaching that "we have the discretion to do or not to do a certain act," but this does not take into consideration the human condition. We are powerless over addictions. To simply slam into sin and tell ourselves, "It is wrong," piles up guilt but does not change our behavior. This is a harsh enslavement to the burden of the law. The spirit of the law is this noticing and responding earlier and more frequently to the impulse of grace.

Humility holds the inner consciousness gently, strives toward the good, and follows the gentle invitation toward God's way. The door is through practice, retraining our mind to consciously follow the pace of grace by noticing the earliest risings of our inclinations and/or replacing our temptations toward selfishness with ceaseless prayer and selfless service.

In Scripture there is a list of virtues, but there is not a method to learn how to practice the virtues, nor is a method taught of how to learn the *praxis* of refraining from the afflictive thoughts. Scriptures are teachings, directives. We need teachers and training of our minds to follow those directives. The positive *praxis* is not a virtue, as in kindness, simplicity, or meekness, but a prayer. The *praxis* is ceaseless prayer. Then, the virtues spring up and the grace needed for the situation is available. So discernment is about noticing sources of thoughts: God, self, or evil. Be vigilant and conscious of inner stirrings of the heart. Know and feel the initial risings of inclinations. Then, follow those subtle impulses toward God. The technical language in the tradition for this practice is "to seek God."

We refrain from evil, turn the self toward God, and let prayer rise. When there's a God-thought that is not sourced in the self or evil, we stand in awe and adoration. No further thought is needed or possible. Pure prayer.

We also need to have discernment (*discretio*) to recognize the comings and goings of our insights and to distinguish temptations and false lights among the true lights that come from God.

Discernment is the attention to the Holy Spirit who teaches us to pray our heart afire. To not be like Jonah requires much work and the grace of God. It does come to completion, however, since this is a revelatory text that mediates an encounter with God. The fourth voice is that wonderful exchange! Actually, it was a gift for me that Jonah was so reluctant. He helped me to see myself. Sinners are my teachers. I want to be like the humble citizens of Nineveh: they heard the word of the Lord and repented. They changed their lives and were saved!

Summary of the Third Dimension of *Lectio Divina*: The Moral Voice Is Heard by the Personal Senses

The literal voice heard by the logical mind is the dynamic of study, research, thinking through the plain explanation of the text. The symbolic voice that uses allegory, metaphors, and literary devices to evoke the meaning is received by the intuitive senses of the reader. The moral voice that dictates action to root out sin, to refrain from self-indulgence, or even evil deeds is received by the personal senses that practice ascetical work to shift the mind toward God. This third dimension is most difficult and takes a lifetime. This is where we live each day as we awake and work out our salvation. This chapter provides some tools and teachings from the tradition. In my *lectio* on the book of Jonah I continue to do that interior work, striving against the afflictions of anger and vainglory. I continue training my mind in the practices of the Jesus Prayer, recollection, colloquy, and the Little Way.

Discernment accompanies me with *lectio* on the book of Jonah with multiple insights around these questions: Who is Nineveh to me? When, where, with whom do I speak? What do I say? What is the word of the Lord that he wants me to articulate or share, and how? Books? E-mail? Web? Visits? Telephone calls? This is an ongoing effort and daily opportunity to live into my faith. I never consider myself proficient but always a beginner who is never surprised when I learn more and more about parts of me still needing the light of grace and the patient glance of our Lord as I commend my soul to him each night before sleep.

Lectio divina is personal prayer, a place to live in this world at this time. It has no apostolic agenda of the reader but much apostolic impulse and guidance from the Holy Spirit. It is God who gives the agenda, the cause, and the situation that sends Jonah.

The fourth dimension I seldom teach anymore because this really happens without us. This experience of God is a promise, and we can expect to know God in our earthly lifetime. In the final vow ceremony we chant, "Accept me, O Lord, according to thy Word and I shall live, and let me not be confounded in my expectations."[29] We expect the mystical relationship with God through Christ Jesus in this lifetime. I find more and more that this is not limited to nuns but available to men and women of all walks of life. Our heritage is a realization of our life with God, as if we were lovers. If one enters this fourth dimension of the mystical, spiritual direction is necessary because it is in this zone that self-deceit rises. Thomas Merton wrote:

> It is necessary to have discernment (*discretio*) to recognize the comings and goings of the Spouse, and to distinguish temptations and false lights among the true lights that come from God. As we grow in experience, we develop the use of the spiritual senses which give us a kind of experience of ineffable and divine realities, sight for contemplating supra-corporal objects, hearing, capable of distinguishing voices which do not sound in the air, . . . smell which perceives that which led Paul to speak of the good odor of Christ; touch which St. John possessed when he laid his hands upon the Word of Life. The spiritual senses do not develop unless we discipline the carnal senses.[30]

Chapter 6

Encountering God:
The Mystical Voice Is Received
by the Spiritual Senses

In the fourth sense, we experience the mystical encounter with God. We return to *lectio divina* with the book of Jonah with the fourth dimension: the mystical voice is received by the spiritual senses.

The fourth dimension of the revelatory text is an encounter for the one who hears that voice. This hidden and subtle voice is heard in the stillness realm of the spiritual senses. For the Jonah *lectio*, this is the experience in the belly of the whale. We have all been there, in exile. While being swallowed up is full of terror, the fear subsides and gives way to that spaciousness that transforms abyss into peace. There are many descriptions of the mystical voice. Similar terms, though differing in languages, are used by mystics in both the East and the West to describe mysticism. We are in the realm of a teaching that, if you have the experience, you do not need to know any more about it and, if you have not had the experience, these descriptions might seem trite or, at best, understated.

It is best not to speak much of this level, so I'll simply share the list and have a concluding paragraph. Most days I do not abide in this fourth voice. I can only report that I am content to be in that third stage of ascetical work rather than in a fourth stage mysticism. It seems that it is taking me a lifetime to hear and heed.

Again, we return to the revelatory text. Scripture has some mystical language; in the book of Jonah it is in the second chapter's canticle. If you read that canticle not as a physical rescue mission but more as a baptismal catechesis, you see that at the deepest levels it is more than being saved; you see the experience of being swept into the vow of total unity and mystical union.

We enjoy the taste of true sorrow, compunction, and pathos turned to joy. We get stilled in the silence of those three days in the belly of the whale. We try as we might to row our boat the other way but get stormed back into our true selves. We receive more light with each step so we can say with the saints that we literally see the light in the light—one light gives us insight into the next light. This fourth sense is the spiritual senses *par excellence*. There's so much power and universal access to the true, the good, and the beautiful.

Now this story is literally true. I am Jonah, I am Nineveh, and I am the shipmates. To do this practice, I had to stay with the narrative of the book of Jonah for about three months, leaning into to it gently but wholeheartedly. Sustained *lectio divina* using this story is a compelling technology for the spiritual journey.

Indeed, the mystical is more real than the literal because you see, touch, feel, hear, smell "it" as it really is and is now.

The Breakpoint

The fourth voice is the mystical voice received by the spiritual senses. The breakpoint happens. There's no need to work on the mystical dimension if the moral voice is heeded. The mystical springs up when purity of heart emerges. The church was strangely right to insist on keeping the commandments all those centuries. This is the door to purity of heart where the mystical encounter happens and spiritual energy rises.

To give personal examples of these ten mystical experiences would be ahead of my practice, but I have met many mystics who know the experience of God but have little language to name their encounters. Most persons who know they've met God are confident and unafraid. Doubt and inner terrors usually melt in the face of God's presence. The fear of God is more of awe and mystery rather than dread and panic.

Cautions at This Stage in the Practice of Lectio Divina

Being human, we can even at this point deceive ourselves. It might be wise to list a few pitfalls to avoid while doing *lectio divina*.

About Self-Diagnosis and Self-Direction in Service of the Self

In the School of *Lectio Divina* it was difficult to get the students to sit back and wait on the Spirit to reveal to them the event of revelation and what door should be taken (Scripture, nature, or life's experience). It is even more difficult to get them to use the prayer practice that was given them rather than have them sort through the options and select this one and then that one, at will. If we do not wait on the Lord at the very beginning of our prayer as practice, then we will have much difficulty being receptive at this mystical level.

About Self Assessing Self in the Spiritual Life

All sins are a form of blasphemy. We take to ourselves what properly belongs to God who alone is to be glorified and praised forever. When we assess ourselves and report how we are in relationship with God, this can be haughty. How would we know that? We subtly are telling God about how God is. That's not for us to know. While we can notice these progressions, it is best not to be self-conscious about one's progress because we really don't know how we are doing. And it really does not matter that we even know. The benefit of practice is simply to do it. More and more I see the wisdom of Benedict's admonition to his followers to vow *conversatio morum* to the monastic way of life. End of story: simply keep on the journey.

We need to encourage each other along the way, but not with reports of our own lights. They are too sacred to share and the biggest danger is to talk, teach, or write ahead of one's practice. In some of the Buddhist traditions, this is grounds for involuntary dismissal from the monastery, and one must disrobe if found guilty of this infraction.

About Method in the Mystical Life

In Merton's book *Contemplative Prayer*, he argues against a method.[1] He makes a case that anyone who thinks he or she has a method in the Christian tradition is usurping the role of Christ Jesus who is our only teacher, our only guru. Christians would not undergo any other initiation rite into another faith tradition. There is no single method of prayer or meditation in the Christian tradition, but we'd pray in the mainstream of the saints who have gone before us. There is also no Christian tradition of teachers who cultivate followers or disciples and/or who initiate devotees as there is in the Buddhist, Hindu, and Sufi traditions. The *staretz* in the Christian East are the closest cousins. They were elders who prayed ceaselessly in self-acting prayer, could read hearts, and transmitted the teachings of their elders through example, preaching, and hearing confessions of sinners.

Once I asked Abbot Francis Kline of Mepkin Abbey if he taught his monks any special meditation practice. He said no. The inner heart of each monk is so precious; that is his domain. Then, in his office,[2] we talked into the wee hours of a Sunday night about how "maybe it was time to restart the desert tradition and provide more actual direction to our monks and nuns." There has got to be a way to honor each person's distinct call from God and also teach the tradition in such a way that *lectio divina* is practiced seriously and wholeheartedly. We ended the extended conversation with the realization that to teach others we must first start with ourselves.

That's why this book is simply sharing how I do *lectio divina* and how I teach it to others. There are many, many ways of doing *lectio*.[3] I shared with Abbot Kevin at Roscrae in Ireland that I was writing a book on *lectio divina* and he said, "Heavens no! Not another book on *lectio divina*. What we need is someone who does it!" His words gave me courage to simply share how it is with me.

About Moral Life as Constitutive of *Lectio Divina*

This method outlined above is what I understand about how and why John Cassian and St. Benedict recommended renunciation as a way of life. This is why it is critical to restore the ascetical dimension as a constitutive part of the practice of *lectio divina*.[4] The theory of maintaining the third moral dimension is in Henri de Lubac's *Medieval Exegesis*. The teaching of the ascetical life, as in the third dimension of *lectio divina*, is often taught freestanding rather than in the context of the revelatory text. This misses the whole essence of the desert legacy in our foundations for the monastic way of life, East and West. If the moral life is separated from the whole culture of following Christ, we revert to the law-and-order Catholics of the 1940s instead of the people of God, the ecclesial gathering at the eucharistic table. We need to keep the word and deed linked so that we not only hear the right message and do the right deed but also become an embodiment of Christ in our times.

It is when those biblical stories become my own that I walk, stand, and sit with the righteous (Ps 1). We only know the revelatory text if we also do the content in our specific life. Wisdom literature is a report of having done it. When we have done it we grasp the wise saying because we know it already from the inside.

The Christ experience is a total fit with the whole of our experience of life. The Catholic Church is Christian to the extent that it mediates the revelation of Christ to us for our times and our salvation. It is in the practice of *lectio divina* that we recover the church and its mysteries; it is through human forms that we find the sacred and holy.

About Being a Teacher Who Is Freestanding or Who Is Not Connected with a Trusted Tradition

Prayer is so delicate that we should not just make up methods like a teacher does with lesson plans. I am quite aware how harmful it is to just borrow this and that from Buddhist or Hindu practice. We need to ask our Lord what he wants and then do it in that order. At this level, no other method in my mind is necessary or helpful. We discover an inner method of listening and doing what we hear as a directive from the Holy Spirit.

About Sharing Mystical Experiences

The advice from St. Thérèse, a saint who should know:

> I don't want to enter into detail here. There are cer-
> tain things that lose their perfume as soon as they are
> exposed to the air; there are deep spiritual thoughts
> which cannot be expressed in human language without
> losing their intimate and heavenly meanings; they are
> similar to " . . . the white stone I will give to him who
> conquers, with a name written on the stone which no
> one KNOWS except HIM who receives it" (Rev. 2:17).[5]

So, to continue my *lectio* of the book of Jonah in this
fourth dimension, I will reserve the right to not reveal
anything mystical that I can report from experience. It
is not wise to take such intimate touches of the sacred
into a public domain. I will, however, list descriptions
that come from our Christian tradition that might give
the reader a language to put into words some of their
experience.

The following is a range of examples of the mystical
level we find in the revelatory text. There are many other
instances, but for the sake of this book I am listing ten
examples of the mystical voice and the corresponding
spiritual capacity of the contemplative engaged in this
deep—very deep—level of prayer.

The fourth dimension of sustained *lectio divina* is the
mystical voice of the text that is read by the spiritual
senses of the reader.

What Is the Mystical Voice of the Text?

Teaching

Revealed texts of Scripture, nature,[6] or experience have more than a hidden meaning, as in unseen or symbolic. The text itself stores and gives a transmission. This inner dimension of a text actually communicates what it signifies, as in a sacrament. So, God humbles God's self to come to us in the Word, Beauty, Truth, and Goodness or in the heart of a personal experience.

Some Scriptures boldly speak about this intimate relationship, as in the Gospel of John, the Song of Songs, or the letters of St. John. Some lines, parables, events, sayings, or narratives of Scripture only are intelligible if one reads the text as if it were a mystical communication. "The Word was made flesh" or "This is my body given for you" are other examples. There are also the other three dimensions stored in the text as it is, in fact, symbolic, dynamic, and literally true, but more than the other three dimensions, there is an explosion of voice integrating the previous dimensions. The text takes on a whole category of the new—not just a new category added upon the former ways of knowing.

What Are Some of the Spiritual Voices?

The mystical voice is not limited by definitions, as in exegesis, but can be grasped. Let me list at least ten (and there are more) descriptions that point to the revelatory text that comes to us through the mystical voice.

Anagogical

We are lifted up and our soul's ascent is natural and with easy flight. We go from light to light. In the light we see the light. Like vines upon a trellis, we grow along the supporting wall with gentleness and gradual sure-footedness because of this luminosity. Glory shines from within and from without; an effulgence of energy is the nature of this realm of deification.

Eschatological

The "already" of the reign of God is in our midst. There is no more to hope for. Our faith is substance because God is here, now and for all eternity. The "not yet" dynamic is also at work in the text. This voice sustains us so that we move and have our being.

Teleological

The end is perfect in Christ Jesus. Our High Priest has bridged the gap. We are acquitted of wrongdoing and Christ Jesus has taken upon himself our sins. Mercy prevails. This voice welcomes death, as dying has been passed over and only life is now and in the next realm. With the exodus event completed, there is an eternal new "now."

Cosmic

We go above but dwell within the whole of it. This voice is speaking from planet Earth and all the billion spheres of matter, light, energy, and motion spinning in our field of expansion and contraction. This cosmic voice awakens our cosmic consciousness that celebrates our unique place in the universe as distinctively human among the organic and living manifestations of life birthing and dying into ever-new life forms.

Unitive

We experience the single point—that irreducible oneness that has no other—that is mysteriously spoken of as Trinity. Through Christ and in the Holy Spirit we, without losing our personal identities, are taken into this vast shore of one grain of sand. This *theosis* or divinization separates us and binds us back to God. Annihilation is prevented as distinction in the Trinity provides an understanding of God and an understanding of ourselves in God. This is impenetrable, as in mystery. In stillness, this mystery chants and is heard; comingling here! This Christ consciousness is so pervasive that we pass through the low door of humility and take off hats and refrain from any speculation and bow in realization.

Contemplative

Both in the dazzling darkness of the *apophatic* voice and in the intimate, personal conversation of the Holy One we hear the voice of the inner guide. Sometimes it is the wind, the fire, the storm, and the flood and at other times, the whisper. The contemplative voice vibrates at a different frequency than does ordinary sound, sight, and feel. This voice speaks with authority, heart-to-heart. This voice comes through icons, chant, incense, and eucharistic bread and wine. Eventually this voice dances right inside! This *perichoresis*, or indwelling, is an experience of the way it is.

Esoteric

There is something secret about this voice. It is heard by those who already "know" (*gnostic*). Stored in this text is a hidden power to transform any and all who consent and take it to heart. The harvest is ripe, but the laborers are few. The vibrations of calligraphy or illumination go deep, beyond decoration or enhancement. Patterns emerge both in daily consciousness and in sleep's deep dreams that repeat the Good News! Joy is not only our calling but our child.

Transcendent

We take off our sandals because we have our own direct experience, and adoration happens to us. The symbol of the sandal is that we meet God with our living flesh and no dead skin (as in leather) is between us. We bow, prostrate, linger in awe, melting our fear into love. Silence. Ineffable yet known, and we know that we know and are known. Fear of the Lord is felt lovingly.

Ecclesial

Not alone, our body, mind, and soul lie low in prostration. We come together even when only one is in the presence. This dialogue becomes communion. We, in

Eucharist, wash feet. We do this together—the God in us and the us in God (synergy). When we put on the mind of Christ, we join our face with all of whom the Abba says, "I am well pleased."

Universal

The mystery of the whole cannot be fathomed. The ineffable is like a lake with no bottom known, as instruments are too weak to plumb vastness and depth. Such unique plausibility is the voice of the All that no contradictions, debate, or faith claims can master. The whole is greater than the sum of its parts in exponential magnitude. The wonderful works of God exceed imagination and awaken an "is-ness" that satisfies a deep laughter.

The voice of the text quickens the reader. The text is inspired by the Holy Spirit and is from God. We can trust that even if we do not get the message, it is there for us and for our salvation, generation upon generation, everywhere and at all times. Even if never read by a mortal, God is.

What Are the Spiritual Senses of the Reader?

Teaching

The revelatory text has a voice that transmits heart-to-heart or soul-to-soul. Just as the text has a way of speaking in a mystical voice, we, the reader, have a way of receiving the mystical voice. The reader is no longer tethered to the text; instead, the reader feels God is coming directly. The text has plowed our soil, weeded our garden, and watered our receptivity so that we are soft and pliant as rain soaking into a parched earth.

The spiritual senses awaken us to this word, this quickening, this subtle presence, this dazzling light, or this epiphany of love. Words fail, but St. Benedict invites us to listen with the ear of our heart (RB Prol). In chanting the psalms, we feel washed in the baptismal waters. When our body sits still, we taste silence. The spiritual senses are as real as our physical senses. We have senses of the body, and we also have senses of the mind, senses of our soul, and senses of our spirit.

The senses of the body are taste, smell, sound, sight, and touch. The senses of our mind are insight, feelings, fear, dread, desire, and doubt. The senses of our soul are illumination, faith, and capacity for mystery. The senses of the spirit are the gifts of the Holy Spirit: wisdom, knowledge, faith, healing, working miracles, prophecy, distinguishing spirits, and tongues. These senses receive the directives of the Holy Spirit and are in service of the Spirit of God (1 Cor 12).

What Are Some of the Spiritual Senses?

The spiritual senses are sharp and, through grace, grasp the contemplative consciousness that springs up.

Anagogical

We progress from light to light either suddenly as in a flash or gradually in episodic shafts, lights that envelop us into insight upon insight. All the senses from body, mind, soul, and spirit work together unto good. Using the anagogical senses prevents the logical thinking mind from getting stuck in speculation and away from one's realization. Self-centered egoic propensities caused by sin are dissolved and purified. God is at work, and there is the shift from the active ascetical moral effort to the passive experience of receptivity and reciprocity. Rest happens.

Eschatological

Senses have a feel for being mortal and grasping the content of desire because fulfillment is already here. The prayer of quiet knows that this is already *it*. Seek no more, and yet the seeking is the language of lovers already in the grasp of the Beloved. Even in the midst of external and extreme suffering there's that deep-down peace of seeing things as they really are. Mystic substitution for another's suffering seems natural and grace-filled because Christ first loved us. This reign of God is already but not yet. There is an absence of apocalyptic dread. Mercy is expected in hope, and love is known now.

Teleological

The end point is seen, not remotely or held in some vague belief. The destiny has a feel from the inside. My "God form" that is imprinted in the psyche is fitted with sturdy confidence. The third eye opens to see at once all directions and everything gathered together in one shaft of light. The Christ consciousness is an awareness that is abiding and available to stay faithful, vigilant, and in anticipatory yearning:

> While standing at a window in the dead of night, Benedict suddenly beheld a flood of light shining down from above, more brilliant than the sun. The whole world was gathered up before his eyes in what appeared to be a single ray of light.[7]

Cosmic

We belong to a universe within multiple complex universes. We awaken to our unique stature among other living beings. Our consciousness pulsates in rhythm with both the interiority of microscopic matter, energy, and light and also the macro formations ever manifesting to our searching eye. This sense of the cosmos is both humility and *theosis*. We are healed of separation and division as all has place, space, and chaotic patterns of shared meaning. We sense our significance in all the cycles of birthing and dying. Birthing has such a force that we thrive on its energy.

Dying also has a place to "make sense" since it is, just is. Dying is a sweet transformation when rightly held in reverence and respect. The dying senses are a separation that factors out the senses of the body and the mind, and we dwell in the soul and awaken to the Spirit. We literally pass over from death to life. The cosmic sense receives, perceives, and conceives this ongoing birthing of our essence in ever-deeper consciousness. We see the blue earth within and without.

Unitive

To be alone satisfies the thirst of our monastic vocation. To be at one in any moment, at any one place, at any venue or situation. We have senses that know our face before we were born. Our memory of God becomes abiding, forgetting the before and the possibility of loss and disintegration. We are not one but also not two. No need to figure it out either! We sense the Trinity doctrine with "Ah-ha!"

Contemplative

The spiritual senses are sometimes *apophatic*, as in seeing into the mystery of that undifferentiated presence that is something, not nothing. Presence saturates void. Here is a list of some of the contemplative senses.

Smell, and sometimes the spiritual senses are as if smell. We are attracted and follow the scent of the inner life. Prayer is natural, and we seek solitude under the river, swim in silence, and become still in that no-gravity of spaciousness. The smell is that perfume of presence that when inhaled seeps into all our lungs that oxygenate our blood, our life force. Mary of Bethany washed the feet of Jesus with precious oil and dried his feet with her hair (John 12). We breathe and offer our prayer like incense. Taken up, all is holy.

Touch, or the spiritual senses are as if touch, when we feel the gentle loving contact from another that soothes, calms, or embraces us. A touch heals and communicates intimacy. We remain in the grasp of God. We have senses to receive this from the inside. When the spiritual sense of touch is activated, the wounds become hallowed places of refuge rather than hemorrhaging sores. The Beloved Disciple leaned on the bosom of our Lord at the Last Supper. We remain at table and abide in love.

Taste; our spiritual senses as if taste bring our intelligence beyond food for the body or knowledge for the mind. As-if taste nourishes our soul with food that is sourced in Another's strength. Taste is cultivated to come to know ever more and more subtle distinctions and patterns of communication with the Beloved or the Holy One. Sober intoxication prevails. The Martha and Mary story inverts the work of preparing dinner, as in food, to say that Mary has chosen the better part to listen at the feet of the Lord and imbibe the Word so that his flesh is our flesh and his blood is our life force (Luke 10). This inherency satisfies hunger and thirst.

Sight; the as-if sight takes us beyond our ordinary ways of seeing and we behold the Lord, as Mary Magdalene did in the garden. Sometimes this as-if sight is in dazzling darkness that Gregory of Nyssa describes in his retelling of the story of Moses. We also are reminded of Zacchaeus who climbed the tree to catch a glimpse and Jesus "looked up" or Jesus "was seen." Our Lord brought him to his senses (Luke 19). We testify to this new order of living by faith. No debate on beliefs can deter us when we've seen the Lord.

Sound; the as-if sound is that shared Christ consciousness that shifts chatter to and between the self's many voices to the Beloved whom you know as you are known.

> A mighty hurricane split the mountains and shattered the rocks before Yahweh. But Yahweh was not in the hurricane. And after the hurricane, an earthquake. But Yahweh was not in the earthquake. And after the earthquake, fire. But Yahweh was not in the fire. And after the fire, a light murmuring sound. And when Elijah heard this, he covered his face with his cloak and went out and stood at the entrance of the cave (1 Kings 19:11-13, New Jerusalem Bible).

Some translations say "still small voice" (RSV), "a sound of sheer silence" (NRSV), "a tiny whispering sound" (NAB). We get the message that Elijah heard the Lord with his spiritual senses. The sound was subtle, definitive, and transforming.

Veiled; our senses reveal indirectly and from underneath. Sometimes there is the use of *synesthesia* that describes the crossing over of senses that signal the code that all words fail to convey meaning. The meaning is beyond speech. The manifestation is ineffable yet heard, felt, understood, and treasured. A taste of silence echoes in stillness. A glance is a transmission of having been seen before I was born. I have been given a name known only by me and my Beloved in which I hear my vocation: "To everyone who conquers I will give some of the hidden manna, and I will give a white stone, and on the white stone is written a new name that no one knows except the one who receives it" (Rev 2:17).

Esoteric

Immediacy because of purity of heart: Scripture, nature, and experience have an esoteric level of contemplation. This inner dynamism is read by the spiritual senses awakened and prepared by no competing consciousness that comes from the eight afflictions. Purity of heart rises because God's shared life (grace) is who we are, yet many souls miss the mark and all of us fall and get up again. Many are called, but few are chosen.

Transcendent

Right-ordered fear awakens us to the Other and restores our creaturely likeness to God. This capacity for awe, wonder, worship, and adoration shifts beyond rituals, obedience to the law, and fear of the Lord and toward a profound readiness to *conversatio morum* (changing our former way of life). We gladly and joyfully surrender self and have a capacity for selfless service. We sense that the "Wholly Other" loves us with merciful compassion. We extend this unconditional love to others without return to the ego.

Ecclesial

A touch opens ears to hear, eyes to see and heed the word proclaimed in our midst. This sense of "we" is known: *koinonia* is poised for *diakonia*, or community in readiness for service. This Way is church.

Universal

This voice is met by the spiritual sense of profound solidarity. So we are back to the main point of the book of Jonah. All who hear the voice of the Lord and repent are saved.

Summary of the Voices and Senses

The mystical level of Jonah chapter 2, the canticle about being saved, provides a permanent place of refuge. The dry land is literally dry, arid. But there is no resting under the castor oil plant to watch and wait for destruction. No, there is sheer gratitude that all are saved in God's mercy. In this dazzling darkness we see the Light of universal salvation. Silence is the rest of the text. Only emptiness can describe the spiritual senses receiving the mystical voice. Sheer silence says it all!

This contemplative dimension can happen without the previous dimensions, but unless we do the inner work of the previous voices received by the appropriate and corresponding senses, the momentary shift in consciousness will fade and evaporate. Everyone seems to wake up sooner or later, but the ongoing work of *lectio divina* keeps us awake.

Spiritual Direction in the Mystical Dimension

Through spiritual direction we would receive a confirmation if we are called to be more passive. Some are called to rest, as in no method, no thought, and no desires except to seek God. The mystical voice heard by the spiritual senses is not meant to be an extraordinary calling to sanctity. It is certainly more sacred than the literal, the allegorical, or the moral voices of the text. The mystical voice challenges us to use discernment to stay in the middle of hearing the word of God and respond without ego-driven motivations. The symbolic voice is heard by our intuition; we get it in a flash. So there are seldom ways of communicating it to someone else. Humility is our friend. We know that we know, and that's enough for us. Again, this is the strongest reason why our *lectio divina* must have the ascetical dimension: blessed are those with purity of heart, for they shall see God.[8]

How does this all work in everyday rule of prayer?

I do the process of asking the Holy Spirit to come and give me my text. That takes an instant, but I *wait upon* it and ask for a confirming sign. Perhaps this might take a week or so. Then, I set about doing the literal level. This might take a month or two. Then, I take weeks on the second level of hearing the symbolic voice. Those meditations take time and lots of protracted periods to do deeply. This takes me months. Then, the third dimension, the moral level, is really what takes me most deeply into the text. Doing the practices takes time, concerted effort in service of the *lectio*. This makes all the difference. I purify my soul to see what the revelatory text is trying to teach me. My encounters with God are mostly at this moral level—do this or do not do this. I find that the level of ordinary human consciousness of living righteously is what *lectio divina* does for me. The mystical level rises from time to time, but I'm content to walk in faith.

Summary and Conclusion

The last breath before death can be a gasp or a grasp. To ensure that we are in the grasp of God, the daily practice of *lectio divina* is a wonderful means. In this sense, *lectio divina* is a place to live in this world but also a place to die into the next.

The literal voice is known by the logical mind and has the effect of calming any confusion. The paradox of opposites is a satisfactory resolution to perplexities. The symbolic meaning evokes intuition through the artistic mediums laced in the text. These insights give confidence to our mind that needs to trust the reality of our perception. The moral clarity can *whisper* rather than shout a steady direction toward God. With the directives, we can gentle into a rhythm of right action. And, finally, in the mystical place, we are inextricably connected to God. Mystical voice summons the spiritual senses, being-to-being. Our relationship is personal and autonomous so that we can bow or, better still, prostrate before our Creator whom we love with our whole heart, mind, and soul.

We greet social opportunities to become a people of God. Our personal invitations seem natural because our hearts are enlarged. We lovingly and compassionately follow the impulses for selfless action without the drag of resistance because sin has been rooted out and ceaseless prayer has been stitched in. Our apostolic outreach is from within and confirmed from without by legitimate authorities of the church, community, or intentional faith community.

We live content with our present situation. Others will see in us the face of humility, but what we are doing is this sustained *lectio divina* every day when we are not doing something else. This is our preferred culture and helps us to live in this world while not being of it. Through sustained *lectio divina* we sustain a Christ consciousness.

Discovering the Next Text

So am I ready for another text? Have I finished the book of Jonah? There might be another theme rising on the horizon. My main theme of Jonah weaves in and out, and then I can expect a new line shimmering in; after much dance and many modulations, the new theme will replace the old melody line. All seems fitting and nothing is lost of the previous text, but a new one deserves my fresh and total attention.

Epiclesis

Let's return now to our original prayer of *epiclesis*. We invoked the Holy Spirit to come, and this Holy Spirit actually came. The mystical teachings about God can be found in the catechesis about the Holy Spirit. When the Spirit comes, we have our own experience of those energies that are the Presence. Jesus came and is still present in these Holy Energies (Holy Spirit). There are some patterns in Scripture that often happen to us too: a second baptismal experience or the gift of tears. There are many symbols for this experience of God: dove, fire, wind, gifts, Paraclete, overshadowing, new garden, torch of the heart, breeze of new life, waters quickened, etc.

All these images evoke the Real Presence, especially when we participate in the sacrament of the Eucharist. This is not symbolic language, not a sign. This is literally a transmission of the energy of God. We go full circle. Literal becomes true! The gift of Holy Spirit is all gift. The heresies that went sideways about work, sex, food, elitism, authority, or Gnostic secrecy served to dismiss Christian openness to the Spirit's coming and being with us today. The Spirit quickens individuals as well as the ecclesiastical community.

A mystic who has had an experience of the Holy Spirit makes for eloquent preaching and teaching. Without this experience speculative reason dominates. Evil spirits are also as real as the Holy Spirit, and the evil spirits can deceive a sincere one who is attached to having experience of mystical levels. The Holy Spirit casts out evil, and one can trust that in this lifetime one can have a sincere and real presence of the Holy Spirit.[9]

The spiritual senses are what the person employs to experience the gifts of the Holy Spirit. These gifts are normal for ordinary Christians and not special for saints of times past. We prayed for the Holy Spirit to come. We renounced sin in order to be ready for this New Life that is actually our original baptismal life in Christ Jesus. We met Jonah, whose name is a derivative of the name "dove," sent by God! There are no limitations to where, how, to whom, how deep, and how pervasive is the Holy Spirit.[10]

Prayer need not be difficult. The method shared here brought forward from our tradition is only one way. Notice the wisdom of the four voices and the human resources (senses) to receive all four voices with complete assimilation and partnership. The revelation of God to the creatures made in the image and likeness of our Creator is the music of this way of prayer. The monastics have kept it from obscurity but it is a treasure for all believers. While it might seem a tough curriculum to learn, is there any better use of our time and talent than to know God now? In this little book, we used Jonah to take us down, down, down to the depth of prayer, and we return on dry land with eyes wide and clear like a child.

The cover of this book is the burning bush. When we listen with the ear of our hearts through *lectio* on Scripture, root out our afflictions, and replace them with ceaseless prayer, stillness rises where there was once agitation and fear. We kneel before our encounter with God. From time to time we can actually see our own light. We have a light of presence, just as God comes in the glory of luminosity. This light, when we are very still and at peace, is blue, the color of the clear sky.[11] This experience of our own sky inside is where ordinary *lectio divina* can take us. This stillness is not just a calming of our thoughts but soundness in body and slow rhythm of heart and breath. But more than this physical and mental peace comes an emotional tranquility that comes from a healthy soul.

Staying with a sustained *lectio*—all the way through the literal voice received by the logical senses, through the symbolic voice recognized by the intuitive senses, through the dynamic moral voice heeded by the ascetical senses that personally takes action on behalf of the word that was revealed by the text—we arrive at that place of rest and stillness, centered in space and time, at home in this world, one with the blue sky above and the blue light emanating from within. This is a prayer that helps us have a holy place to live in this world at peace and full of love.

Conclusion

To look one last time at the book of Jonah: How did the *lectio* become the revelatory text? Did I hear it? It is too soon to report great lights or accomplishments. And I am not sure that anyone would see grace at work in himself or herself. But there are a few indicators to share that this sustained method of *lectio divina* is worthy of a lifetime.

From the literal study using my logical mind I found the skillful use of Jonah's story impacted me more than thousands and thousands of pages of other books. I delved into the questions with simple answers. I could readily satisfy my questions by checking out the footnotes and annotations in my Bible. The study was enjoyable and gave me a sense of pride in my heritage as a Judeo-Christian woman.

The second level of exploration moved me deeply into all the symbols and hidden meanings. This took me further than I have ever gone into mystery with humor, content, and context. I got not only Jonah's story but my own as well. I am that same reluctant prophet, those same Ninevites in need of repentance.

The third level is to do the right things with the effort. I am still at work hearing the moral imperatives that keep coming and coming to me as I do more and more to uncover my flawed psyche. There is no way to communicate how grateful I am that afflictions that have burdened me for years have mercifully been lifted through the ascetical practices. I still am in the grasp of an affliction of anger or depression from time to time, but it passes quickly and dissolves into a compuncted memory. I can honestly say those afflictions, for the most part, have been extirpated (rooted out) and not only leave peace where anxiety or rage reigned but have been replaced at the conscious level with an abiding consciousness of the Presence.

And, finally, the mystical voice is mostly a soft, still silence. I need some monastic forms that protect me from returning to my former way of life, for my "former way of life" is the way I lived before I did the practice of *Lectio Divina*. This encounter with God is life, lived in love, with a long, lingering gaze before my revelatory text—the burning bush. This Presence has a knowing closeness with Jesus. The soft, still voice has the feel of the Holy Spirit. There's a "we" that faces our loving Abba/Father. I have found my place in this world. I have found an idiom (the burning bush) that describes *lectio divina*.

What now? Am I still doing *lectio* through the revelatory text of the book of Jonah? No. Now, I am doing *lectio continuae*, which is a slow lingering listening of the whole Bible, book by book, starting with Genesis. It is taking me years. I have at least another year or two before I end with the book of Revelation, but I am in no hurry. *Lectio* is what I do when I am not doing anything else, or is it that I kneel before the burning bush as I do that something else?

And what about the method presented above? Am I doing each book using the four voices received by the four senses? Yes, but the sequence is not linear. It's more of a circle or a sphere with my time mostly doing the third dimension of the moral voice heard by my personal senses. The method doesn't matter. What matters is the burning bush. And from time to time I am called to hold open that page in the *lectio continuae* and check out another text. I'm slowly doing an immersion into the text of Vatican II. I've read books by Yves Congar and am pacing myself through the documents of Vatican II. No rush, and many pleasant surprises that our very human church has such possibility of joy these next fifty years.

Appendix

Catechesis on Confession[1]

Catechesis on Confession

The Rite of Reconciliation presumes a life directed toward God. From time to time, we stray and need correction to return to our heart's desire. To have a traditional practice that provides this reorientation is a gift to reorder our lives.

To progress in the spiritual life we need to start over. To break the chains of our past way of living this amazing ritual of confession has power and grace. The ritual is simple, but profound.[2]

The Sinner[3] Does Some Interior Work Examining His or Her Consciousness[4]

Climate: quiet, at peace. Have an image of our Lord before you. Lay aside any anxiety and allow thoughts and feelings to rise. This is the opportunity to repent, to be acquitted of the burden of sin. To be forgiven and to do penance is a sign of a restored confidence in God's mercy.

Take the posture, like the Orthodox, with the priest by the side of the penitent and the sinner kneeling before the icon of Christ Jesus. The sins are confessed to God. The priest witnesses and admonishes and gives absolution in the name of Jesus.[5]

Perform an examination of consciousness, looking at what's on my mind and weighs heavily in my heart. Imagine Jesus before you: "Listen! I am standing at the door, knocking; if you hear my voice and open the door, I will come in to you and eat with you, and you with me" (Rev 3:20).

Five questions should come to mind:[6]

1. When, what, and how did I stray from my mindfulness of you?
2. When and on what occasions do I forget you?
3. What habits of selfishness are sinful for me?
4. What do I need to confess and be forgiven so that I may start again?
5. Do I need to make amends? Whom have I hurt? Am I sorry?

Read one of the gospels and linger over the incidents in which Jesus forgave sins, healed infirmities, and admonished sinners.

Naming the Matter to Confess

The sinner prepares a short list to confess. Sin is defined using three criteria:

1. Serious matter: we knew it was wrong (could be a thought or a deed)
2. Freedom of choice: we were free to do otherwise but did it anyway. This option could have been omission or commission.
3. Did the evil: we did what was wrong and it harmed self or others. This could be in the mind only, or it could also be sin of omission, not doing what we could and should have done.

Contrition

We are sorry for what we have done and desire forgiveness from God and from others. This is remorse, having a contrite heart. We might have profound understanding of how we got into the mess, but nevertheless we did not withstand the test of temptation and refrain from acting out the wrong choice.

Confessing to a Priest[7]

We are willing to tell our sins out loud to a priest, who in the name of Christ Jesus mediates the forgiveness of our sins. This telling to a human is a human way of expressing our sorrow and the willingness to repent and convert our lives back to a holy relationship with God and each other.

Receiving a Penance

We go into the confessional or wherever the priest is ritually prepared to hear our confession. We confess and receive a penance. This penance is a symbolic act that demonstrates our willingness to accept being forgiven and to start over with our lives and resist temptation and sin. This penance could be a prayer or a reading of Scripture or an act of sacrifice like making restitution. It is done outside of the ritual time of confession.

Act of Contrition

Make an act of contrition, which is a prayer asking for God's forgiveness. It could be the Our Father or the Lord, Have Mercy or the standard Act of Contrition we use at Eucharist:

> I confess to almighty God
> and to you, my brothers and sisters,
> that I have greatly sinned,
> in my thoughts and in my words,
> in what I have done and in what I have failed to do,
> through my fault, through my fault,
> through my most grievous fault;
> therefore I ask blessed Mary ever-Virgin,
> all the Angels and Saints,
> and you, my brothers and sisters,
> to pray for me to the Lord our God.

And the priest says:

> God, the Father of mercies,
> through the death and resurrection of his Son
> has reconciled the world to himself

> and sent the Holy Spirit among us
> for the forgiveness of sins;
> through the ministry of the Church
> may God give you pardon and peace,
> and I absolve you from your sins
> in the name of the Father, and of the Son
> and of the Holy Spirit.

The person says, "Amen."

Receive Absolution

The priest then gives absolution. This prayer is profound. The sins are not only forgiven but also absolved. This means the sins are taken away from the person's record before God. There are many erroneous teachings about punishment due to sin. Most of these teachings were meant to give the sinner confidence in God's mercy, but instead there were literal pictures of hellfire and damnation. Reading the healing stories of Jesus in the gospels we know that he simply said to go in peace and sin no more!

When I teach this I say that we are not only absolved but also acquitted. Our sin is taken away. The church, through the priest's words of absolution, officially declares that we are not going to have to be punished even though we might be guilty of the charge. Our past is expunged. It is as if we did not do it. We are free of the obligation that our sins deserve. God removes our sin (and guilt) as far away as the east is from the west. This is good news! With this acquittal we can start over with full energy and grace toward God and the good.

The Catholic tradition has total trust in the redemptive event of Jesus Christ dying on the cross and taking upon himself all our sins. This is grace upon grace and the Good News. We are to have faith, repent, and believe in the Gospel and share this good news.

Making Amends

We, for our part, still feel inclined to make amends and do so not out of guilt but out of justice and right order. Making amends also is a good retraining of the habits that caused our sinfulness in the first place. Sometimes these amends are more symbolic than actual. We might make a contribution to a charity or do that outreach to our elderly relations to signal conversion from a relationship in our past that we regret.

Prayer for Healing

We pray for God's healing of any part of us still feeling the effects of sin.

Compunction

We pray for the gift of compunction. This remorse is helpful to prevent sin. We even ask for the gift of tears to soften our hard hearts. Compunction is a feeling of sorrow.

Pray for **Penthos**

We pray and cultivate the abiding sense of being in need of God's mercy. This is the virtue of *penthos*.[8] We long for God and feel our distance because of being a sinner; at the same time, we have an intense sense of God's love. This living into the mercy of God is called *penthos*.

Ceaseless Repentance

Ceaseless repentance is a practice. We must do our part in crying out for God's mercy. This is an amazing grace. When we have the practice of ceaseless repentance, we do not sin because we do not go up the chain of temptation that causes us to sin. Instead, we ceaselessly recite the Jesus Prayer: Lord, Jesus Christ, Son of the Living God, have mercy on me, a sinner.

Afterword

Much has been written in recent years about *lectio divina*, reviving a method of prayer used by Christians from the earliest centuries well into the late Middle Ages. One cannot help but be grateful for this comprehensive contribution toward our understanding of the practice, this means of encounter with the Divine.

What Sister Meg Funk has done in her book is not only to describe the encounter but to provide a step-by-step exercise in the art of sacred reading. She gives us a practical training, a living experience of becoming adept with this method of prayer. In doing so, she has used one of the best tools we could hope for from a writer: her lived experience. Clearly, *lectio* has informed and transformed her life. There is nothing so enriching, so life-giving, as the shared life experience Meg has done here with great openness and transparency. Again, one is left with a sense of gratitude.

To lead us on this journey of deepening *lectio* experience, Sister Meg has used the book of the prophet Jonah.

One may wonder about the reasons of her choice, but as her treatise has unfolded, one is left with not only a new appreciation of the prophet but a growing awareness of how much our lives are concealed and revealed in this inspired text. To get sidetracked with doubts about its historicity would be to have missed the power of its message. Meg does not do this but has led us through it into whole new layers of consciousness, designed to leave us with a lasting sense of surprise at our human depth and capacity for the Divine.

This may best be illustrated in how she speaks of the "concentric structure of the scenes within scenes [that] is like a modern art film: instead of going up to Nineveh, Jonah goes down to Tarshish, then down to Joppa, down into a ship, down into the hold, and, finally down to the bottom of the sea and into the belly of a great fish. The countermovement is the sailors' fear of the storm, which becomes a great fear and then a religious fear (awe)."

What Meg has done is take us into the depths of our experience throughout her book, opening our hearts to a new and transformative encounter with the living God. She knows all too well how this encounter may be blocked by our fears and thus has challenged us to let them be turned into religious awe.

To pave the way into the religious encounter deep down within, *lectio divina* needs to be closely associated with the rest of our lives, with the whole environment around us so that it is fed and nourished by it. It is here, it seems to me, that Meg may be doing us the greatest service, leading us into a final integration where nothing may be left hidden from the presence of the living God. We may have found ourselves frightened at the prospect. But then again Meg eases the burden by reminding us that this is really not our own doing but God's, bringing about a Christ consciousness within. Provided we allow the deep down of our lives to be opened, grace floods in with unexpected encounter.

She has done this by taking us through the fourfold senses or voices of Scripture that open onto a confession of our total dependence on God; onto the training of the mind; into the practice of virtue; into the awareness of generational sin; into the value of the cell, our manual labor, and even the clothing we wear. The discipline of being attentive of our thoughts as they arise, so highly esteemed by early desert experience, is further refined by an excellent exposé on discernment. She then shows how this way of prayer has borne abundant fruit in the lives of many holy women and men throughout the ages.

Amid all this, one is left with a vibrant sense of a lived experience, the beauty of a human life that has slowly unfolded, blossomed before the living God, the subconscious revelation of a gifted writer. This work will bear fruit in many lives for years to come.

Michael Casagram, OCSO
Novice Master
The Abbey of Gethsemani

Notes

Iconographer's Preface

1. "God became human so that human beings may become God" (St. Athanasius). For the Eastern fathers, the formulation of the doctrine of deification affirmed the reality of humanity's innermost hope as "belonging to God." St. Gregory Nazianzus argued that the root of a person's true greatness and calling lay in being "called to be a god." Elsewhere, St. Basil the Great insists that "the goal of our calling is to become like god." The ultimate redemptive destiny of humanity is none other than to attain likeness to God and union with him. Deification denotes a direct union and a total transformation of the human person with the living God by divine grace. St. Basil the Great says that human beings are nothing less than creatures that have received the order to become gods. The descent (*katavasis*) of God has offered the created order the capability of ascending (*anavasis*) to the Divine in the Holy Spirit. For the Eastern fathers, deification is God's greatest gift to, and the innermost goal of, human existence. Although the term does not occur in the Holy Scriptures, the Greek fathers believed that it was a fitting theological term affirming the command of 2 Pet 1:4, that is, "to become participants of the divine nature."

2. See Phil 1:9-10.

3. Literally: "He [God] rested from all his work which God created to do or make" (Gen 2:3b).

4. See Exod 3:7-10.

Introduction

1. Pope Benedict XVI, addressing participants of the International Congress on the fortieth anniversary of *Dei Verbum*, Rome, September 16, 2005, *Dei Verbum Bulletin* 76/77 (2005): 5.

2. See *Rule of St. Benedict 1980* (*RB 80*), ed. Timothy Fry (Collegeville, MN: Liturgical Press, 1981). There are fourteen references to *lectio/lectio divina* in the Rule.

RB Prol 1: Listen carefully, my son, to the master's instructions and attend to them with the ear of your heart. This is advice from a father who loves you; welcome it, and faithfully put it into practice.

RB 4.55–58: Listen readily to holy reading, and devote yourself often to prayer. Every day with tears and sighs confess your past sins to God in prayer and change from these evil ways in the future.

RB 9.8: Besides the inspired books of the Old and New Testaments, the works read at Vigils should include explanations of Scripture by reputable and orthodox catholic Fathers.

RB 21.4: They are to be chosen for virtuous living and wise teaching, not for their rank.

RB 48.1: Idleness is the enemy of the soul. Therefore, the brothers should have specified periods for manual labor as well as for prayerful reading.

RB 48.4: From the fourth hour until the time of Sext, they will devote themselves to reading.

RB 48.5: But after Sext and their meal, they may rest on their beds in complete silence; should a brother wish to read privately, let him do so, but without disturbing the others.

RB 48.10: From the first of October to the beginning of Lent, the brothers ought to devote themselves to reading until the end of the second hour.

RB 48.13: Then after their meal they will devote themselves to their reading or to the psalms.

RB 48.14: During the days of Lent, they should be free in the morning to read until the third hour, after which they will work at their assigned tasks until the end of the tenth hour.

RB 48.23: If anyone is so remiss and indolent that he is unwilling or unable to study or to read, he is to be given some work in order that he may not be idle.

3. Henri de Lubac, *Medieval Exegesis: The Four Senses of Scripture*, vols. 1 and 2 (Grand Rapids, MI: William B. Eerdmans Publishing, 1998). These two volumes are almost one thousand pages of text and notes. I have read them carefully three times to get a sense of this masterful resource. Henri de Lubac, a twentieth-century scholar and participant of the *Resourcement* Movement, compiled in a compelling way the whole development of how the senses of Scripture are to be understood and taken seriously as a contemplative support for *lectio divina*.

See also R. McNally, "Medieval exegesis," in Catholic University of America, *New Catholic Encyclopedia*, vol. 5 (Palatine, IL: Jack Heraty & Associates, 1981), 707–12. This is a shorter summary that reports the demise of the hermeneutics that dominated Western theology until about the year 1500. The five-page article ends with this sentence:

With the coming of the Reformation and humanism, which employed the disciplines of the new learning, criticism, philology, and history, the usefulness of medieval exegesis as a hermeneutical system was virtually terminated. Face to face with this new critical spirit and its scientific technique, medieval exegesis ceased to be relevant and was discarded. (712)

This article gives a sketch of how the sense theory evolved. Sometimes it was threefold body, soul, and spirit anthropology with a threefold sense of Scripture: somatic, psychic, and pneumatic (Origen, *De Principiis* 4.2.4). John Cassian teaches the threefold method, using the terms "letter" or literal "*tropicus*," which is the moral sense, and higher understanding, which is called "anagogic" (*Collationes* 8.3). Gregory the Great, in his homilies on

Ezekiel (*Hom*. 9, n.8), developed the fourfold senses theory: literal and three spiritual senses (allegorical, moral, and anagogic). The literal was not neglected, but the spiritual meanings were the revelation (708).

4. Today we know so much more about the brain, the mind, and the way different parts of the brain have different functions. The logical mind is located in the left hemisphere. The symbolic functions of the mind are located more in the right hemisphere. We now have much research to train the mind to refrain from destructive emotions that harm self or others. This is the classical ascetical, moral character training. When we train our thoughts, we train the mind, combined with bodily exercise, to have benefits beyond former expectations. Our personal senses have programs that require direct practice to unlearn rote behaviors and learn preferred ways of acting. The spiritual senses are now being discovered by research into quantum physics. This book can only point to some of this exciting research, but it intends to teach the distinctiveness of each of the senses proper to the voices received in the practice of *lectio*. I recommend Mind and Life Institute, University of Wisconsin–Madison Center for Creating a Healthy Mind, Forgiveness Education sponsored by Fetzer Institute (www.fetzer.org). Also, a movement in this direction is initiated by Karen Armstrong: www.charterforcompassion.org.

5. The metaphor of under the river and above the river is used here to describe our interior life of the spiritual journey under the river that we cannot see from the surface of the river. Above the river where boats glide is the external journey. See my book, *Into the Depths: A Journey of Loss and Vocation* (New York: Lantern Books, 2011), for my major immersion experience under the river in Bolivia.

6. About the term "sustained" in this *lectio*: Many people I listen to are doing a sustained encounter with news or interpersonal conversations with friends. Their default culture is secular. The

way I understand *lectio* is to have one's revelatory text as default, where I go when I'm not doing anything else.

7. David G. R. Keller, *Oasis of Wisdom: The Worlds of the Desert Fathers and Mothers* (Collegeville, MN: Liturgical Press, 2005). For a concise description of the Catechetical School of Alexandria, see 18–19.

8. Sandra Schneiders, "Scripture and Spirituality," in *Christian Spirituality: Origins to the Twelfth Century*, ed. Bernard McGinn, John Meyendorff, and Jean Leclercq (New York: Crossroads, 2000), 1–20. This initial chapter in the volume sets out the delicate negotiations of the Christ event in human history: a Jewish Christ in the midst of a Greek culture that evolved into a dominant Latin church.

9. I was traveling from Beech Grove to Saint John's in Collegeville, Minnesota. We were hosted for an overnight at Holy Wisdom Monastery of Madison, Wisconsin. I took time in their monastic library and found one of the books attributed to the author of the *Cloud of Unknowing*. His usage of Middle English was translated to use the word "voice" when it was the word spoken from the text of Scripture and the word "senses" when it referred to the reader's reception of the voice. So this had been done in English as early as the latter half of the fourteenth century. I find this distinction sharpens the way we listen to the text. It is confusing when we use the word "senses" for both the levels of meaning of the text and the ways of interpretation of the listener of the text. We know that the level of the text requires a corresponding level for the reception of the text. In literature the genre dictates the skill sets of receptivity on the part of the reader.

10. The Pontifical Biblical Commission, *The Interpretation of the Bible in the Church* (Boston, MA: Pauline Books and Media, 1993), 126. This directive says that *lectio divina* can also be a common prayer form. I find in the Rule of Benedict that he uses the word *collatio* for reading in common, not *lectio*.

11. International Commission on English in the Liturgy, *The Roman Missal, Third Edition* (Collegeville, MN: Liturgical Press, 2011).

12. Interdicasterial Commission, "Epiclesis," in *The American Catholic Catechism* (Ligouri, MO: Ligouri Publications, 1994), par. 1105.

13. RB Prol 4: First of all, every time you begin a good work, you must pray to him most earnestly to bring it to perfection.

14. This was a life-changing event for me. With the grace of God I literally reversed the habit of indiscriminate reading.

15. What translation of a Bible should be used for *lectio divina*? I recommend four translations for Catholic readers: The New Revised Standard Version (NRSV), the New American Bible, Revised Edition (NABRE), the Jerusalem Bible (JB), and the New Jerusalem Bible (NJB).

My favorite translation is the Jerusalem Bible. It is translated from original languages into French and then into English. I find the Jerusalem text more poetic, and it sounds true to my ears. I also think the Jerusalem Bible editions have taken much trouble to format and leave some white spaces for just resting with a text. The NJB has several editions that are easy to hold and pleasant to read.

The most recommended translation today is the New Revised Standard Version (NRSV). It is excellent and has study editions like the New Oxford Annotated Bible. The NRSV has attended to inclusive language.

I use a hardback NRSV Catholic Edition plus Anglicized Text and the Revised Standard Version Catholic Edition (RSV) from Oxford University Press for both travel and at home for study and teaching, but for days of retreat I use my Jerusalem Bible that I got as a present from my mother at first vows in 1963.

For *lectio divina* we need a translation that is from original languages, as in formal correspondence. We also need a Bible with footnotes, commentary, and study guides.

For more information on choosing a Bible translation, do an online search for John J. Pilch. Or see the pamphlet: John J. Pilch, *Choosing a Bible Translation* (Collegeville, MN: Liturgical Press, 2000).

16. Guigo II, *The Ladder of Monks and Twelve Meditations*, trans. Edmund Colledge and James Walsh, Cistercian Studies Series 48 (Kalamazoo, MI: Cistercian Publications, 1981). Written by a Carthusian in the twelfth century, this is a classic in Western Christian mysticism. Today the most common method in use is the four steps outlined by Guigo II, who wrote *The Ladder of Monks* a thousand years after the teachers of the Alexandrian School of Catechesis. Guigo II provides a masterful outline of reading, meditating, praying, and *contemplatio*. No distinctions are made between the voice of the text and the senses of the reader. *Lectio* is simply to read the text four different times using different approaches. This risks either reading the text with a personal agenda or only grasping the literal level four different ways. Also, this method of *lectio divina* was never meant to be done in common (as a group prayer) or at one single session (like morning prayers before the Blessed Sacrament).

Chapter 1

1. This translation by Laurence O'Keefe, OSB.

Chapter 2

1. Abraham J. Heschel, *The Prophets* (New York: Harper and Row, 1962), 401, n. 84. Sackcloth was the symbol of repentance. Sometimes this is a haircloth used as a sign of mourning. For the Gentiles to appropriate this symbol of repentance would have been repulsive to Jonah, a devout Jew.

2. Anthony R. Ceresko, "Jonah," in *The New Jerome Biblical Commentary*, ed. Raymond Brown, Joseph Fitzmyer, Roland Murphy (Englewood Cliffs, NJ: Prentice Hall, 1990), 380.

3. The great fish was not a whale as we typically understand the term. The second, informal definition of a whale is an impressive, very large, or very enjoyable example of something. This second definition is the whale of the book of Jonah used symbolically.

4. *The Complete Parallel Bible* (New York: Oxford University Press, Inc, 1993). NSRV is New Revised Standard Version; REB is Revised English Bible; NAB is New American Bible; NJB is New Jerusalem Bible.

Chapter 3

1. Benedicta Ward, *Harlots of the Desert: A Study of Repentance in Early Monastic Sources*, Cistercian Studies Series 106 (Kalamazoo, MI: Cistercian Publications, 1987). Ron Pepin and Hugh Feiss, *Saint Mary of Egypt: Three Medieval Lives in Verse*, Cistercian Studies Series 209 (Kalamazoo, MI: Cistercian Publications, 2005). These two delightful books contain early monastic stories, which speak of God's presence and work in the lives of those who repent.

2. "[The abbot] is believed to represent Christ in the monastery, for he is called by his name in accord with the saying of the Apostle: 'You have received the Spirit of adoption of children, in which we cry: "Abba, Father!"' (Rom 8:15)" (Terrence Kardong, *Benedict's Rule: A Translation and Commentary* [Collegeville, MN: Liturgical Press, 1996], 47).

3. John Chrysostom, *On the Incomprehensible Nature of God*, trans. Paul Harkins, Fathers of the Church, vol. 72 (Washington, DC: The Catholic University of America Press, 1984). This new translation captures the wit and wisdom of St. John. These homilies are word wonders that capture the audience with profundity and humor.

4. Paul Murray, *A Journey with Jonah: The Spirituality of Bewilderment* (Blackrock, Co. Dublin: Columba Press, 2002). This book is a delightful sustained meditation on the book of Jonah. In this readable little book of seventy pages, which includes the NAB version of the Jonah text, Murray makes a compelling case that Jonah is in all of us and gives us insight and flight from our bewilderment.

5. Ibid., 23. A quote from Paul Murray's wonderful study of Jonah:

Modern consciousness, Buber writes, looks to the soul as the only sphere in which we can expect to harbour or discover the "divine." And this marks, of course, a complete shift away from transcendence to immanence. In Buber's opinion, "(Modern consciousness) will have nothing more to do with the God believed in by the religions, who is to be sure present to the soul, who reveals himself to it, communicates with it, but remains transcendent to it in his being." A spirituality of this kind—an exclusively *immanent* spirituality—at least in its extreme manifestations, represents a regress back to a safe, controlled environment, a return to "the womb" even. In terms of religion, it is nothing less than a spiritual manifestation of "the Jonah syndrome."

Chapter 4

1. Jean Leclercq, *The Love of Learning and the Desire for God: A Study of Monastic Culture.* (New York: Fordham University Press, 1961). This book was published the year I entered the convent (as it was called in those days). In reading this book I understood for the first time that the culture of the monastery is *lectio divina*. Each monastic is doing his or her *lectio* and sustaining a God consciousness. Without the practice of *lectio divina*, we simply take on another culture, for example, a university, a hospital, a hotel, a cottage industry, a farm, etc.

2. Kallistos Ware, *The Orthodox Way* (Crestwood, NY: St. Vladimir Seminary Press, 1999), 123: "Normally three levels or degrees are distinguished in the saying of the Jesus Prayer. It starts as 'prayer of the lips,' oral prayer. Then it grows more inward, becoming 'prayer of the intellect,' mental prayer. Finally the intellect 'descends' into the heart and is united with it, and so the prayer becomes 'prayer of the heart' or, more exactly, 'prayer of the

intellect in the heart.' At this level it becomes prayer of the whole person—no longer something that we think or say, but something that we are: for the ultimate purpose of the spiritual Way *is* not just a person who says prayers from time to time, but a person who is prayer all the time. The Jesus Prayer, that is to say, begins as a series of specific acts of prayer, but its eventual aim is to establish in the one who prays a *state* of prayer that is unceasing, which continues uninterrupted even in the midst of other activities."

3. Archimandrite Nektarios Antonopoulos, *Return: Repentance and Confession; The Return to God and His Church* (Akritas Publications, 2002). This eighty-six-page book from the Orthodox tradition helped teach me more about repentance than about sin and moral degrees of gravity. The point is Christ, and sin separates us from our own presence and the Presence of Jesus, our Lord. Repentance is the way back through the door of mercy. This return has a tradition through the sacrament of confession.

4. The word "mantra" is not universally accepted for naming the repetitive use of a word or a phrase used to become ceaseless prayer. In East–West dialogue with Hindus and Buddhists we seem to be talking about the same thing, but I can also be sensitive to the fact that the Christian Orthodox might not feel comfortable with the use of the word "mantra." There are differences in the initiation rite where the guru gives the disciple his or her particular mantra and the baptismal rite where the priest presides in the name of Christ.

5. Thomas Hopko, *Sin: Primordial, Generational, Personal*, cassette (Crestwood, NY: St. Vladimir Seminary Press).

6. There are three areas of contemporary research that I read but have no competence to teach: brain science, quantum physics, management through strengths based on natural talent. These three fields of study are optimistic about the human condition and have practical implications for education and spirituality. I recommend several sources for follow-up studies.

On training of the mind: S. Begley, *Train Your Mind, Change Your Brain* (New York: Ballantine Books, 2007); J. Taylor, *My Stroke of Insight: A Brain Scientist's Personal Journey* (New York: Plume, 2006); J. Mcquaid and P. Carmona, *Peaceful Mind: Using Mindfulness and Cognitive Behavioral Psychology to Overcome Depression* (Oakland, CA: New Harbinger Publications, Inc. 2004).

On quantum physics: B. Chase and M. Vicente, *What the Bleep!? Down the Rabbit Hole* (Beverly Hills, CA: Quantum, 2006), DVD. This three hundred–minute, three-disc special edition can be found on www.whatthebleep.com. What is significant is that classic physics was the worldview of religion. Spirituality always did know this other realm. Now the new physics is naming it and wondering in the mystery!

This training of the mind is His Holiness the Dalai Lama's main teaching. I recommend his books and audio CDs: *How to Practice: The Way to a Meaningful Life* (New York: Simon & Schuster, 2002), disk; *Destructive Emotions: How Can We Overcome Them?* (New York: Holtzbrinck Publishers, 2003), disk; *The Universe in a Single Atom, The Convergence of Science and Spirituality* (New York: Random House Audio, 2005), disk. See also R. Mehrotra, *The Essential Dalai Lama: His Important Teachings* (New York: Penguin Books, 2005).

On management: D. Clifton and P. Nelson, *Soar with Your Strengths* (New York: Dell Publishing, 1992); M. Buckingam and D. Clifton, *Now, Discover Your Strengths* (New York: Free Press, 2001).

While *penthos* and humility is a healthy place to live as a mortal, when "at work in the world" this mindfulness must be tempered with an awareness of one's strengths and talents. In management, it is best to gravitate toward one's strengths and gifts in self and others. In the 1970s I trained with Selection Research Incorporated using Donald Clifton's insights. His daughter, Connie Rath, was my mentor. SRI acquired Gallup Organization. I recommend the two books just cited that are currently available. There's no duplicity in this approach. Ever mindful of being in need of God's mercy we gladly offer our gifts for the sake of others.

7. Athanasius, *The Life of Antony and the Letter to Marcellinus*, trans. Robert C. Gregg, Classics of Western Spirituality (New York: Paulist Press, 1980). Antony lived from AD 251 to AD 356 in Egypt. He left his home and sold all to the poor to become a monk in the desert. His biography, written by Athanasius in AD 357, is a classic of Christian literature and inspires the flowering of the monastic movement even today.

8. Letters of St. Vincent de Paul, referenced in current Constitutions of Daughters of Charity (May 1, 2004).

9. "On his way there Benedict met a monk named Romanus, who asked him where he was going. After discovering the young man's purpose, Romanus kept it secret and even helped him carry it out by clothing him with the monastic habit and supplying his needs as well as he could" (Gregory the Great, *Life and Miracles of St. Benedict: Book Two of the* Dialogues, trans. Odo J. Zimmermann and Benedict R. Avery [Collegeville, MN: Liturgical Press, 1949], 4).

10. "Melania got Evagrius to promise to adopt the monastic life, and she promised to pray for his healing. He recovered quickly. According to Palladius, he 'received a change of clothing at her hands'" (William Harmless, *Desert Christians* [New York: Oxford University Press, 2004], 314).

11. A defining characteristic of poverty is the scarcity of discretion. The poor have few options.

Chapter 5

1. For myself, since my community does not wear the habit these years I have dressed as simply as possible. No one can dress up like a nun on their own initiative. It is given from one who has gone

before you. In my lifetime, we have implemented the directives of Vatican II. Perhaps the next generation can reclaim the practice of a portable cell without wearing a dress that symbolizes power, control, and otherworldliness.

2. John Cassian (c. 360–430) influenced St. Benedict, who quotes him over 150 times in his Rule. Cassian was from Dacia (today's Romania) and joined a monastery in Bethlehem. From there, he traveled to Egypt, visiting the desert elders and recording their wisdom in his two books: *The Institutes* and *The Conferences*. He founded his own monastery in Marseilles, France. His writing provides the theory that supports the story of Antony's leaving all and living the monastic way of life.

3. See my *Thoughts Matter: Discovering the Spiritual Journey* (Collegeville, MN: Liturgical Press, 2013). This book is recommended for all the eight thoughts and their teachings.

4. I use the word "mind," not just our brain. New research and these ancient teachings locate the memory in every cell of our body. We need to learn where anger is stored, back it out, and relearn a loving response.

5. A rule for Orthodox nuns, written by the same nuns who live it! Orthodox Nuns of Holy Myrrhbearers Monastery, Monastery Typicon (rule approved by the bishop), Otego, New York. Used by permission of Mother Raphaela.

We also need to learn to understand the passions, which sometimes inform our conduct in ways that are not in accordance with our prayer, reading, and conversations with our mentors. Anger, for example, is a passion that can quickly destroy both friendships and community life in a monastery. How we approach anger, especially in ourselves and in others, is therefore critical to our life. St. John Climacus and other monastic writers tell us that one of the signs of a monastic is lack of anger. The psalmist, on the other hand, tells us to "be angry, but sin not."

We will all be tempted by feelings of anger at one time or another, some to a greater or lesser degree. One who cannot be responsible for the way she displays her anger, however, should learn humility from the fact that she does not have the self-control that St. Paul tells us is one of the fruits of the Holy Spirit.

6. Irenee Hausherr, *Spiritual Direction in the Early Christian East*, Cistercian Studies Series 116 (Kalamazoo, MI: Cistercian Publications, 1990). This is the best source for this early tradition of manifestation of thoughts to a wise elder.

7. This anagogic principle sounds sublime: in the light you see the light. But it happens in ordinary things too. I recently cleaned my cell, wrote six letters, and cleaned off e-mail. Then I saw a new, clear directive of different things that needed careful and prayerful attention.

8. See my *Tools Matter: Beginning the Spiritual Journey* (Collegeville, MN: Liturgical Press, 2013), 82. Thoughts have an anatomy from beginning to end: included here are teachings from both Evagrius and from John Cassian on the *logismois*.

When seekers would go to a desert elder, they attended to the movements of the heart (of the mind), suggestions, inner prompting. When such an impulse or inner prompting develops into an outward deed, into consent of the will, it would be too late to show all this to the director.

One must then go to a confessor and resolve not to wait until next time. Elders differentiated between moments of temptation. There is the suggestion in thought (*prosbole*), which is free from blame (*anaitios*). Next follows the coupling (*syndiasmos*), an inner dialogue with the suggestion (temptation), then the struggle against it (*palë*), which may end with victory or with consent (*synkatathesis*), actual sin. When repeated, such acts produce a passion (*pathos*), properly speaking, and, in the end, a terrible captivity of the soul (*aichmalosia*), which is no longer able to shake the yoke of the Evil One.

The proper object of *exagoreusis tön logismön* (revelation of thoughts) is the first stage of this process, the *prosbole*. One must crush the serpent's head as soon as it appears. . . . All this is done through an entire strategy: *nepsis* (vigilance), watchfulness, the guarding of the heart (*custodia cordis*) and of the mind, prayer, especially the invocation of the name of Jesus, and so forth. (Hausherr, *Spiritual Direction*, 157)

The theory is that our thoughts loop around and hook us. We can watch our thoughts (*nepsis*) and see the points of contact, invitation and consent of the will. Some thoughts are slicker and more insidious and catch us before we catch them. We need help. It's good to speak our thoughts to a wise elder who can (a) receive our thoughts/urges; (b) give us the opportunity for honesty and truth bearing; (c) help us notice when we get hooked and take action that is against our best self; and (d) help us to notice the content of the thought (e.g., food, sex, things, etc.) and also the stage of the thought, the consent, the patterns of *pathos*.

9. R. French, *The Way of a Pilgrim and the Pilgrim Continues His Way* (San Francisco: Harper Collins, 1965). This little edifying morality tale is an excellent teaching tool. This is teaching through a story. It seems also to have the power of transmission. Those who read it prayerfully feel the graces of an elder, soul to soul.

10. We must respect the Orthodox reluctance to share this sacred and ancient prayer form. The risk of someone misusing the prayer, using the sacred name of Jesus, is of concern. Western practitioners tend to isolate the practice from the full membership with obligations in the church and therefore take it out of the context that provides safeguards to prevent pride. The prayer has the content of humility, so the disposition of *penthos* is essential.

11. St. Nikodimos of the Holy Mountain and St. Makarios of Corinth, *Philokalia: The Complete Text*, vols. 1–4, ed. G. E. H. Palmer, Philip Sherrad, and Kallistos Ware (London: Faber and Faber,

1979–95). An anthology of the spiritual writings of the early fathers. This is the primary source for all the teachings on the Jesus Prayer.

12. Kallistos Ware, "Ways of Prayer and Contemplation," in *Christian Spirituality: Origins to the Twelfth Century*, ed. Bernard McGinn, John Meyendorff, and Jean Leclercq (New York: Crossroad, 2000), 395–414. This encyclopedic entry is a comprehensive history, theory, and scholarly presentation of the Jesus Prayer. Kallistos Ware is a master teacher who writes technical research for lay readers. The Jesus Prayer is not a movement but a deeply embedded tradition of a sturdy contemplative practice available to all Christians.

13. I. Brianchaninov, *On the Prayer of Jesus*, trans. Fr. Lazarus (Boston and London: New Seeds, 2006). This is the classic guide to the practice of unceasing prayer as found in *The Way of a Pilgrim*. This small, readable book not only is helpful for teaching about the Jesus Prayer but has directives for those who have practiced the Jesus Prayer for some years. The chapters on various Orthodox teachers provide comprehensive summaries. The chapters on the many issues about the Jesus Prayer and prayer of the heart for spiritual directors are essential reading for this practice.

14. Daniel Chowning, "Jesus Christ, Friend and Liberator: The Christology of Teresa of Jesus," in *A Better Wine: Essays Celebrating Kieran Kavanaugh, OCD*, ed. Kevin Culligan (Washington, DC: ICS Publications, 2007), 3–63. There are three major themes in the life of Teresa. She was born in 1515 and entered the monastery at the age of twenty-one; in 1545 she had an encounter with the risen Lord, and in 1556 Teresa had definitive conversion experience of Jesus. Her doctrine on the humanity of Christ has implications for her spirituality. Our relationship with the risen Christ has implications.

15. See ibid., 18–20.

16. See Teresa of Avila, *The Book of Her Life*, in *The Collected Works of St. Teresa of Avila*, trans. Kieran Kavanaugh and Otilio Rodriguez, vol. 1 (Washington, DC: ICS Publications, 1976).

17. Karl Rahner, *Foundations of Christian Faith* (New York: Seabury, 1978), 309.

18. See Teresa of Avila, *The Book of Her Life*, 191–200, and St. Teresa of Avila, "The Interior Castle," in *The Collected Works of St. Teresa of Avila*, trans. Kieran Kavanaugh and Otilio Rodriguez, vol. 2 (Washington, DC: ICS Publications, 1980), 263–452.

19. For further reading on the practice of colloquy, see my *Discernment Matters: Listening with the Ear of the Heart* (Collegeville, MN: Liturgical Press, 2013), 102–7.

20. For further reading on the practice of the Little Way, see ibid., 107–18.

21. John Cassian, *The Conferences*, trans. Boniface Ramsey, Ancient Christian Writers 57 (New York: Newman / Paulist Press, 1997). John Cassian, *The Institutes*, trans. Boniface Ramsey, Ancient Christian Writers 58 (New York: Newman / Paulist Press, 2000).

22. Scripture quotations in this section are taken from the *New American Bible with Revised New Testament and Revised Psalms* © 1991, 1986, 1970 Confraternity of Christian Doctrine, Washington, DC.

23. Since writing *Lectio Matters* I have written a full book on discernment, but to reflect the full-blown method of *lectio divina* from the Alexandrian tradition, our good works and our ascetical life is constitutive of *lectio*. The moral life cannot be separated from prayer.

24. This section on evil is from conversations with Msgr. John Ryan (d. 2005). He was the exorcist for the Archdiocese of Indianapolis. I'd have him come to my class and teach this area from his many years of experience.

25. For the Catholic teachings on ontic evil, see the *Catechism of the Catholic Church*.

26. In *Discernment Matters* I reduce the seven steps to five so people can keep the steps in mind, but I'm leaving the original text here for the sake of learning the sequence of the method.

27. Brother Lawrence of the Resurrection, *The Practice of the Presence of God*, trans J. Delaney (New York: Image Books, 1977), 79.

28. See my *Discernment Matters*.

29. RB 58.21, quote from Psalm 118:116.

30. Thomas Merton, *Cassian and the Fathers: Initiation into the Monastic Tradition*, ed. Patrick F. O'Connell, Monastic Wisdom Series 1 (Kalamazoo, MI: Cistercian Publications, 2005).

Chapter 6

1. Thomas Merton, *Contemplative Prayer* (New York: Image Books, 1971), 34; Thomas Merton, *The Inner Experience: Notes on Contemplation* (San Francisco: HarperSanFrancisco, 2003). In his book, *The Inner Experience*, Merton was more insistent on the formation of contemplatives. His reservations about method were more of a critique of the mental prayer meditation sessions held in common rooms where there is a passage and a point to think about. Merton was into reforming the monastic culture so that monks had the kind of time for prayer that could go deeper and deeper. Divine Office is so rigorous and manual labor was so intense there was little quality time for *lectio*. This fed Merton's intense desire to become a hermit.

2. Abbot Francis had a practice of inviting his special guests for these conversations. He'd have a bottle of quality wine and a glass of water for each of us. He also served gourmet nuts and chips.

3. Francis Kline's *lectio* is in his book *Lovers of the Place: Monasticism Loose in the Church* (Collegeville, MN: Cistercian Publications, 2012).

4. John Cassian, "Fourteenth Conference: On Spiritual Knowledge," in *The Conferences*, trans. Boniface Ramsey, Ancient Christian Writers 57 (New York: Newman / Paulist Press, 1997), 515.

5. *The Autobiography of St. Thérèse of Lisieux: Story of a Soul*, trans. John Clarke, 3rd ed. (Washington, DC: ICS Publications, 1996), 77.

6. K. P. Kramer, *Martin Buber's I and Thou: Practicing Living Dialogue* (Mahwah, NJ: Paulist Press, 2003). Buber has a great description of a Doric pillar:

> Out of a church wall in Syracuse, in which it had once been immured, it first came to encounter me: mysterious primal mass represented in such simple form that there was nothing individual to look out, nothing individual to enjoy. All that could be done was what I did: took my stand, stood fast, in face of this structure of spirit, this mass penetrated and given body by the mind and hand of man. Does the concept of mutuality vanish here? It only plunges back into the dark, or it is transformed into a concrete content which coldly declines to assume conceptual form, but is bright and reliable. (62)

Kallistos Ware, "Ways of Prayer and Contemplation," in *Christian Spirituality: Origins to the Twelfth Century*, ed. Bernard McGinn, John Meyendorff, and Jean Leclercq (New York: Crossroad, 2000), 395–414:

> They came to the righteous Anthony one of the wise men of that time and said: "How ever do you manage to carry on, Father, deprived as you are of the consolation of books?" He replied: "My book, philosopher, is the nature of created things, and it is ready at hand whenever I wish to read the words of God." (398)

7. Gregory the Great, *Life and Miracles of St. Benedict: Book Two of the Dialogues*, trans. Odo J. Zimmermann and Benedict R. Avery (Collegeville, MN: Liturgical Press, 1949).

8. It is tempting here to write a teaching from Cassian on pure prayer based on the teachings of Evagrius. This simply would be intellectual content for me to share and very far from my experience. I do recommend three books that review that literature with

great insight: William Harmless, *Desert Christians: An Introduction to the Literature of Early Monasticism* (New York: Oxford University Press, 2004); Columba Stewart, *Cassian the Monk* (New York: Oxford University Press, 1998); David G. R. Keller, *Oasis of Wisdom: The Worlds of the Desert Fathers and Mothers* (Collegeville, MN: Liturgical Press, 2005).

9. J. Breck, *Scripture in Tradition: The Bible and Its Interpretation in the Orthodox Church* (Crestwood, NY: St. Vladimir's Seminary Press, 2001), 195–210. In chap. 11, "Jesus Christ: The 'Face' of the Spirit," there is a wonderful meditation on how we understand the distinctions between Jesus and the Holy Spirit. The author's *lectio* on the Spirit in the Old and New Testaments is thorough and helpful.

10. S. Burgess, *The Holy Spirit: Eastern Christian Traditions* (Peabody, MA: Hendrickson Publishers, 1989).

11. Harmless, *Desert Christians*, 353:

Evagrius sometimes said that the mind "sees its own light." In one key passage, he gave a more precise explanation: "When the mind—after having stripped off the old man—has been reclothed in the (new) one who comes from grace, then it will see its state, at the moment of prayer, similar to sapphire or to the color of the sky."

Appendix

1. The Rite of Reconciliation that includes confession of sins is the Catholic sacrament. I'm avoiding that term so that all sinners can avail themselves of this tradition and know their sins are forgiven.

2. Paul Turner, *Preparing for Confession: Receiving God's Mercy* (Chicago: Liturgical Training Publications, 2005). I have found this little thirty-page pamphlet to be a comforting aid for new and old sinners coming to this ancient sacrament. It is well worth the price.

3. I've been asked if Christians can delete the word "sinner." No. To live into our whole myth system and beliefs we are the creatures

and God is the Creator. The word "sin" and the acceptance of my human condition as a sinner gives me a relationship with God, ground under my feet, and peace of heart. To miss sin gives me no door for reconciliation for myself and compassion for others.

4. I am deliberately using the word "consciousness" rather than the word "conscience." When we examine our conscience we tend to find acts of sinfulness. Consciousness is a larger word to express the undifferentiated afflictive patterns. This early monastic tradition is a sturdy way of life that keeps one's attention on God and how thoughts matter. We catch the thought early, often, and deliberately. This inner work prevents sin. We see that consciousness rather then conscience is our object of concern even for confession of sins. Conscience focuses on sin. Consciousness focuses on God.

5. P. Harrilchak, *Confession with Examination of Conscience and Common Prayers: Way to a Common Growth in the Spirit of Repentance* (Reston, VA: Holy Trinity Orthodox Church, 1996).

6. In writing this examination of conscience, I took three days to list all the sins according to each of the eight afflictive thoughts (see *Thoughts Matter*). Then I realized that in the gospels Jesus was total compassion. He simply healed people, forgave them, and said to sin no more. It is not sin but our relationship with God that is at issue here.

7. Given the shortage of priests today in retreat centers, parishes, hospitals, and Catholic social service centers, there's the need to confess when there is no priest available. I recommend that spiritual elders simply receive the confession and pray with the person. We suggest that when they have an opportunity to participate in the rite of reconciliation with an ordained priest they simply name their sin and ask for formal absolution. God's mercy prevails. Pastoral sensitivity guides each situation.

8. Irenee Hausherr, *Penthos: The Doctrine of Compunction in the Christian East*, trans. Anselm Hufstader, Cistercian Studies Series 53 (Kalamazoo, MI: Cistercian Publications, 1982).

Select Bibliography

The Art of Prayer: An Orthodox Anthology. Compiled by Igumen Chariton of Valamo. Translated by E. Kadloubovsky and E. M. Palmer. Edited by Timothy Ware. London: Faber and Faber, 1966.

Benedict of Nursia. *RB 1980: The Rule of St. Benedict in Latin and English*. Edited by Timothy Fry. Collegeville, MN: Liturgical Press, 1981.

Bianchi, Enzo. *Praying the Word: An Introduction to* Lectio Divina. Translated by James W. Zona. Cistercian Studies Series 182. Kalamazoo, MI: Cistercian Publications, 1998.

Billy, Dennis J. *The Way of the Pilgrim: Complete Text and Reader's Guide*. Liguori, MO: Liguori Publications, 2000.

Brother Lawrence of the Resurrection. *The Practice of the Presence of God*. Translated by J. Delaney. New York: Image Books, 1977.

Bossis, Gabrielle. *He and I*. Translated and condensed by Evelyn M. Brown Sherbrooke. Quebec: Mediaspaul, 1969.

Burton-Christie, Douglas. *The Word in the Desert: Scripture and the Quest for Holiness in Early Christian Monasticism*. New York: Oxford University Press, 1993.

Casey, Michael. *Sacred Reading: The Art of* Lectio Divina. Liguori, MO: Triumph Books, 1995.

———. *Toward God: The Ancient Wisdom of Western Prayer*. Rev. ed. Liguori, MO: Triumph Books, 1996.

Cassian, John. *The Conferences*. Translated by Boniface Ramsey. Ancient Christian Writers 57. New York: Newman / Paulist Press, 1997.

———. *The Institutes.* Translated by Boniface Ramsey. Ancient Christian Writers 58. New York: Newman / Paulist Press, 2000.

Climacus, John. *The Ladder of Divine Ascent*. Translated by Colm Luibheid and Norman Russell. Classics of Western Spirituality. New York: Paulist Press, 1982.

The Cloud of Unknowing and the Book of Privy Counseling. Edited by William Johnston. Garden City, NY: Image Books, 1973.

de Lubac, Henri. *Medieval Exegesis: The Four Senses of Scripture*. Vols. 1 and 2. Grand Rapids, MI: William B. Eerdmans Publishing, 1998.

Funk, Mary Margaret. *Discernment Matters: Listening with the Ear of the Heart*. Collegeville, MN: Liturgical Press, 2013.

———. *Humility Matters: Toward Purity of Heart*. Collegeville, MN: Liturgical Press, 2013.

———. *Lectio Matters: Before the Burning Bush*. Collegeville, MN: Liturgical Press, 2013.

———. *Thoughts Matter: Discovering the Spiritual Journey*. Collegeville, MN: Liturgical Press, 2013.

———. *Tools Matter: Beginning the Spiritual Journey*. Collegeville, MN: Liturgical Press, 2013.

Gregory of Nyssa. *The Life of Moses*. Translated by Abraham J. Malherbe and Everett Ferguson. Classics of Western Spirituality. New York: Paulist Press, 1978.

Gruen, Anselm. *Heaven Begins within You: Wisdom from the Desert Fathers*. Translated by Peter Heinegg. New York: Crossroad, 1999.

Guigo II. *Ladder of Monks and Twelve Meditations.* Translated by Edmund Colledge and James Walsh. Cistercian Studies Series 48. Kalamazoo, MI: Cistercian Publications, 1981. A new translation by Sr. Pascale-Dominique Nau was published by lulu.com, 2012.

Harmless, William. *Desert Christians: An Introduction to the Literature of Early Monasticism*. New York: Oxford University Press, 2004.

Hausherr, Irenee. *Penthos: The Doctrine of Compunction in the Christian East*. Translated by Anselm Hufstader. Cistercian Studies Series 53. Kalamazoo, MI: Cistercian Publications, 1982.

à Kempis, Thomas. *Imitation of Christ.* Translated by Wm. Creasy. Notre Dame, IN: Ave Maria Press, 1989.

Laird, Martin. *Into the Silent Land*. New York: Oxford University Press, 2006.

Leclercq, Jean. *The Love of Learning and the Desire for God: A Study of Monastic Culture*. Translated by Catherine Misrahi. New York: Fordham University Press, 1961.

Masini, Mario. *Lectio Divina: An Ancient Prayer That Is Ever New*. Translated by Edmund C. Lane. New York: Alba House, 1998.

McGinn, Bernard. *The Presence of God: A History of Western Christian Mystery*. Vol. 1: *The Foundations of Mysticism: Origins to the Fifth Century*. New York: Crossroads, 1991.

Merton, Thomas. *The Climate of Monastic Prayer*. Cistercian Studies Series 1. Kalamazoo, MI: Cistercian Publications, 1973.

Pelikan, Jaroslav, *Whose Bible Is It? A Short History of the Scriptures*. New York: Penguin Books, 2005.

Pennington, M. Basil. *Lectio Divina, Renewing the Ancient Practice of Praying the Scriptures.* New York: Crossroad, 1998.

Philokalia: The Complete Text, vols. 1–4. Compiled by St. Nikodimos of the Holy Mountain and St. Makarios of Corinth. Translated and edited by G. E. H. Palmer, Philip Sherrad, and Kallistos Ware. London: Faber and Faber, 1979–95.

Salvail, Ghislaine. *At the Crossroads of the Scripture: An Introduction to* Lectio Divina. Translated by Paul C. Duggan. Boston: Pauline Books and Media, 1996.

Spidlik, Thomas. *The Spirituality of Christian East: A Systematic Handbook*. 2 vols. Translated by Anthony P. Gythiel. Cistercian Studies Series79. Kalamazoo, MI: Cistercian Publications, 1986.

Stewart, Columba. *Cassian the Monk*. New York: Oxford University Press, 1998.

Stinissen, Wilfrid. *Nourished by the Word: Reading the Bible Contemplatively*. Translated by Joseph B. Board. Liguori, MO: Liguori Publications, 1999.

Studzinski, Raymond. *Reading to Live: The Evolving Practice of* Lectio Divina. Cistercian Studies Series 231. Collegeville, MN: Cistercian Publications, 2009.

Teresa of Avila. *The Way of Perfection: A Study Edition*. Edited by Kieran Kavanaugh. Translated by Kieran Kavanaugh and Otilio Rodriguez. Washington, DC: ICS Publications, 2000.

Thérèse of Lisieux. *Story of a Soul: The Autobiography of St. Thérèse of Lisieux.* Translated by John Clark. 3rd ed. Washington, DC: ICS Publications, 1996.

The Wisdom of the Desert. Compiled by Thomas Merton. New York: New Directions, 1960.